MW00915314

ALL ABOUT EDEN

The Genesis of *Sex*

H. HIRSCH COHEN

Suite 300 - 990 Fort St
Victoria, BC, V8V 3K2
Canada

www.friesenpress.com

First Edition — 2021

ISBN
978-1-5255-7486-3 (Hardcover)
978-1-5255-7487-0 (Paperback)
978-1-5255-7488-7 (eBook)

1. RELIGION, BIBLICAL CRITICISM & INTERPRETATION, OLD TESTAMENT 1

Distributed to the trade by The Ingram Book Company

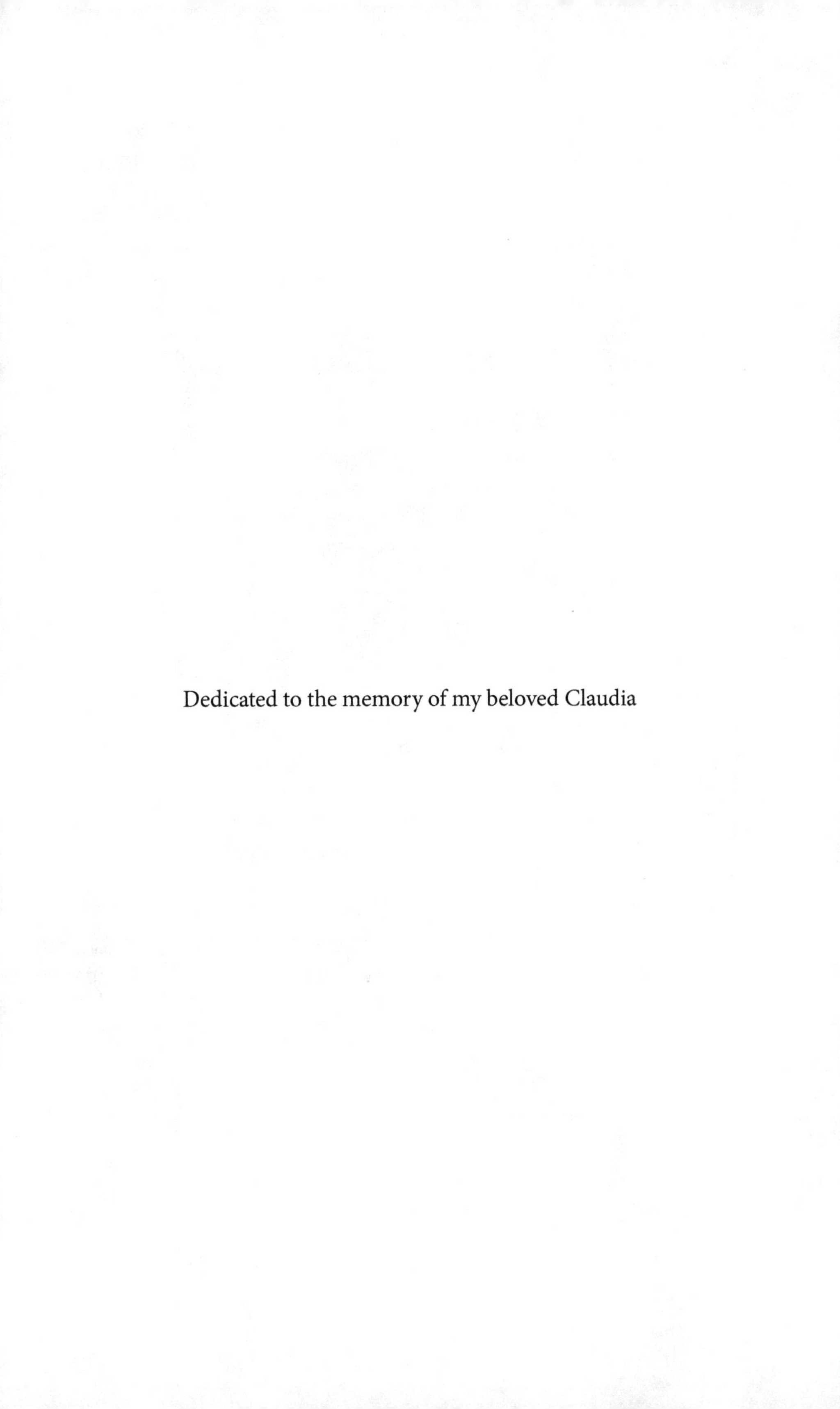

Dedicated to the memory of my beloved Claudia

CONTENTS

PREFACE

In a cartoon in The New Yorker,[1] Adam, sitting with Eve under a fruit tree, says: "I can't help thinking there's a book in this."

Prescient Adam. Only it's not a book, it's books—thousands upon thousands of books, all centered on what is probably the best known, but least understood, story in all of Western civilization.

The misreading of the Garden of Eden story, according to Harold Bloom in The Book of J, stems from the many thousands of exegetes who have read this "ironic narrative as a story of sin or crime and its appropriate (or incommensurate) punishment" (178). In my reading of the Hebrew text of Genesis 1–3, I find nothing that speaks of sin or punishment, because Eve and Adam have done nothing that merits punishment.

To the contrary, they comply fully with God's directive that they attain the fertility to procreate—"be fruitful" (Gen 1:28). How they become fertile is the subject of Genesis 2–3. Once Eve and Adam become fecund, they must leave the garden; however, their departure is not to be construed as a punishment. Rather, it is God's way of safeguarding Eve and Adam from a calamity of untold proportions were they to remain in the garden.

I arrived at these conclusions after reexaminating the meanings of key Hebrew words in Genesis 2–3. What necessitated such a reevaluation is the Hebrew word pakach, "to open," as used in connection with the eyes of Eve and Adam (Gen 3:7). Its meaning introduced me to a story that knows of no walking, talking snake, and no tree of knowledge of good and bad. Admittedly, there is a walking, talking creature in the garden, and, yes, it engages Eve in conversation, but it is not a snake. Moreover, neither God nor this creature misleads Eve about what to expect after she eats the fruit of a certain tree. That Eve should bear the onus of having introduced death into the world is not the point of the story. Indeed, it is to misread it completely. Rather, the objective of the narrator is to present an account of how Eve and Adam become procreative.

My interpretation of Genesis 2–3 obviously deviates from the institutionally entrenched traditions with which we are all familiar. Unfortunately, it will not be the first time that established traditions have obscured the meaning of the biblical text. By challenging these traditions, no matter how firmly embedded in the common mind, I hope to persuade the daughters of Eve that their foremother was honored and respected as the coequal of Adam.

ACKNOWLEDGMENTS

The phrase "It takes a village" is factually true in my case, because it really took a village to help me complete this book. I live in the village of Centerville, in the town of Barnstable, on Cape Cod. While Centerville has a small library, it can boast of a dedicated interlibrary loan department that compensates for its size. It is this department that eased the transition from Storrs, Connecticut to Centerville, Massachusetts. Though retiring to the Cape meant having to do without the resources of a large university library, the Centerville librarians offset this loss with interlibrary loans, which, over the course of two decades, must have been in the hundreds. The one drawback was the waiting period: it was not unusual to wait a month or two for the requested book to arrive. The late Phyllis Byan set the standard for processing my requests, and this tradition of excellence has been maintained by Linda Cardone, who continues to work wonders. To Linda and the librarians who preceded her, I offer heartfelt thanks. I also must mention my indebtedness to Caroline Reed, formerly staff librarian at the Jane Bancroft Cook Library of New College in Sarasota, Florida. Its extensive collection of material on biblical studies and the history of the Near East proved to be most useful, and when I wanted to tap into the internet, there was Caroline, ready to assist.

My dear friend Tom Philbrick, professor emeritus of the English department at the University of Pittsburgh, approached my manuscript with the same insight and editorial expertise that he displays in his exhaustive study of James Fenimore Cooper. Specifically, I wanted to know if Tom, as representative of the reader without any knowledge of Hebrew, could follow my interpretations. The answer is yes. He not only understood my interpretations, but he also alerted me to passages that called for clarification. For Tom's assistance I remain deeply indebted. I also wish to thank David Halperin, professor emeritus of the department of religious studies at the University of North Carolina and author of "Seeking Ezekiel," a compellingly cogent picture of the prophet, for critiquing drafts of selected chapters.

I am grateful to the following exegetes for answering an occasional query: James Sanders, Mark Smith, Carol Meyers, Ian Ritchie, Ronald Veenker, William Schniedewind, Rabbi Henry Cohen, and the late William Hallo, Marvin Pope, and Herbert Chanan Brichto, who encouraged me in my work by stressing that "exegesis is an art, not a science. And one exegesis does not necessarily rule out another one—even if their vectors point in opposite directions." I also wish to thank Dr. Bernard Witlieb for proofreading my manuscript and my brother Arthur E. Cohen, M.D. for answering my questions pertaining to certain aspects of biblical biology. I am grateful to Dr. David Loveman, Dr. William Troetel, and Gary Damiecki, who were on hand to work through the inevitable computer glich. Finally, I wish to express my profound appreciation to my son Douglas for all the time helping me get my manuscript ready for publication. I can not thank him enough for his invaluable assistance.

Unfortunately, my beloved Claudia, who succumbed to a fall three years ago, cannot share with me the satisfaction of seeing our work finally published. I say "our" work, because without her encouragement, I never would have persevered in a project that extended far longer than was ever anticipated—a period of well over two decades.

ABBREVIATIONS

ANET	Pritchard, James B., ed. Ancient Near Eastern Texts Relating to the Old Testament. 3d ed. Princeton: Princeton University Press, 1969.
BCE	Before the Common (or Christian) Era
BDB	Brown, F., S. R. Driver, and C. A. Briggs. A Hebrew and English Lexicon of the Old Testament. Oxford: Clarendon Press, 1929.
CE	Common (or Christian) Era
Jastrow	Jastrow, M. A Dictionary of the Targumim, the Talmud Babli and Yerushalmi, and the Midrashic Literature. 1st ed. 1903. New York: Pardes Publishing House, 1950
JB	Jerusalem Bible
JPS	The Holy Scriptures. Philadelphia: Jewish Publication Society of America, 1917.
KJV	King James Version
K-B	Koehler, Ludwig and Walter Baumgartner. Lexicon in Veteris Testamenti Libros. Leiden: Brill, 1958.
Lewis and Short	Lewis, Charlton and Charles Short. A Latin Dictionary. 1st ed. 1879.Oxford: Clarendon Press, 1962.

LSJ	Liddel, Henry G., Robert Scott, and Henry S. Jones. A Greek-English Lexicon. 1st ed. 1843. Oxford: Clarendon Press, 1961.
NEB	New English Bible, 1970
NJPS	New Jewish Publication Society Bible-- The Torah, 1962, 1978
NRSV	New Revised Standard Version. New Oxford Annotated Bible, 3rd ed. New York: Oxford, 2001.
RSV	Revised Standard Version of the Holy Bible. Oxford Annotated Bible. New York: Oxford University Press, 1962.

TRANSLITERATION OF HEBREW[2]

CONSONANTS:

Except for the silent alef and ayin, the consonants are sounded in their order of appearance in the Hebrew alphabet:

b, v, g, d, h, v, z, ch (like German ch), t

y, k, ch (like German ch), l, m, n, s, p, f,

ts, k, r, s, sh, t

VOWELS ARE SOUNDED AS:

a, ah, as a in cart

ei, as a in hay

e, eh, as e in met

i, as i in bit or ea in beat

o, as o in go

u, as oo in loot

ai, as i in high

INTRODUCTION

The Storyline

In a plot familiar to just about every schoolchild, God creates Adam, then Eve, and places them in a wondrous garden, where they may eat from every fruit tree except one: the tree of knowledge of good and bad. Were they to do so, God warns, they would die on the spot. A sly snake persuades Eve to ignore God's warning. So, she eats the fruit and induces Adam to do the same. God reacts to their blatant act of disobedience not with death, but with banishment: they must leave the garden, never to return. Once settled outside of Eden, Adam will spend his days laboriously clearing the land of thorns and thistles; and Eve, in addition to helping Adam clear the field of rocks, will suffer the pain of childbearing.

The reader must be perplexed by Scripture's treatment of Eve and Adam after Eden, for their purported disobedience is never mentioned again. Claus Westermann writes that "there is no tradition of the narrative of Gen 2–3 throughout the whole of the Old Testament. ... It is not quoted and is never mentioned."[3] And Gary Anderson asks how this story can have "such intrinsic significance and yet be thoroughly ignored by the rest of the Old Testament and the teachings of Jesus."[4]

Prophetic Silence

Most remarkable is the silence of the pre-exilic Hebrew prophets. Given the gender bias of these men—"at times so venomous," writes Ita Sheres, "that some scholars have suggested that the prophets were misogynists"[5]—and given the dominant prophetic theme of the inherent disobedience of Israel,[6] one would think that Isaiah or Hosea would have seized the opportunity to treat Eve as a piñata, reviling her for her disobedience. But nothing of the sort happens. Instead of venomous, virulent attacks, there is only silence. Eve and Adam are never mentioned—and for good reason. By eating the fruit of the tree in the middle of the garden, Eve and Adam are simply complying with God's directive that they acquire the generativity to start populating the earth. That they succeed in acquiring the capacity to procreate is manifest in the "opening of their eyes" (chapter 1). Eve and Adam, told to be "fruitful and multiply" (Gen 1:28), can hardly be faulted for becoming generative. They do what they are told to do. Consequently, Scripture has nothing more to say about them, except to note that the family tree extends to Noah and his three sons (Gen 5). In the centuries following, Eve will be honored as the mother of a line of kings.

The fruit that endows Eve and Adam with procreative fluid comes from the fig tree, "the tree of procreation" (chapter 2). The exquisite aroma of the fig tree convinces Eve of its procreative power, just as fragrance determines royalty in the story of Esther (chapters 4 and 5). Not only do Eve and Adam eat the fruit of the fig tree, but they also utilize the sap of the trunk and the leaves of the tree to keep themselves fully charged with potency for "when the moment is ripe" (chapters 2 and 3).

The Septuagint, the translation of the Hebrew Bible into Greek (third and second centuries BCE), renders the fig tree as "the tree of knowledge of good and bad," because the Jewish translators used alternative definitions of the Hebrew to show that at the beginning of creation, God bestows upon Eve and Adam ethical guideposts that later were to elevate the status of Jews living under the Ptolemies.

The third figure in the garden is not the proverbial sly reptile, but a lecherous man-horse erotically attracted to Eve (chapter 7). The man-horse/centaur urges Eve to eat the fruit of the fig tree, so that Eve, becoming generative, will be driven to have sex with this creature. To foil its scheme,

God transforms the man-horse into a seal that will be confined to a thin ribbon of beach far from human contact (chapters 9 and 11). My reconstruction of the story requires that Eden front a large body of water—the Mediterranean Sea is just such a large body of water—to accommodate the centaur-turned-seal. Doubtlessly, the biblical narrator was aware that the Mediterranean Sea had been home to monk seals up and down the Levant for millennia (chapter 10).

Banishment

Adam, when questioned by God about eating the fruit, blames Eve for doing so (chapter 8). But God is not interested in assigning blame; He simply wants to know if the woman and man have acquired the ability to procreate. Learning that they have, God banishes them from the garden to save them from tragedy; for, if they were to eat the fruit of the tree of life, they would be setting the stage for a Malthusian nightmare, with generations living forever on a starvation diet in an area the size of a postage stamp.

For life after Eden, God clothes Eve and Adam in linen tunics—an investiture that symbolically affirms them as the progenitors of the future kings of Israel (chapter 13). At home in the nearby highlands, Eve and her daughters will experience the "bad" side of procreation: painful delivery, followed by quarantine. That Eve and her daughters will be isolated for a longer period of time following the birth of a daughter (Leviticus 12:2–5) is not to acknowledge the superiority of the male, but rather to protect the mother after parturition from being infected by her husband during coitus. As explained in twentieth-century gynecological literature, the mother needs more time after the birth of a girl than after the birth of a boy to build up the necessary antibodies to counter a possible coital infection (chapter 6). While the ancients may not have been familiar with the concept of antibodies, they certainly knew the benefits of quarantine.

Sexual intercourse, multiple deliveries, and long hours toiling in the field eventually take their toll on Eve. Drained dry of the bodily fluids essential for life, she dies; but unlike the brief reference to Adam's death (Gen 5:5), her death is not recorded. Likewise, a combination of the grunt work of farming and coital exertion will deplete Adam of his life-sustaining fluids (chapter 12). Since no reason is given for Adam's death, I assume the narrator views death as God's way of alleviating the constant tension between population growth and the food supply.[7] Paul Ehrlich's *Population Bomb* apparently has been anticipated by the narrator.

Resolving a Paradox

At first glance there seems to be no logical explanation for two antithetical, yet accurate, readings of Genesis 2–3.[8] The problem is resolved, however, by the dates of composition. The two readings differ, because they were composed at different times, under different circumstances, by different people. The earlier version was written by King Hezekiah's scribes in classical (biblical) Hebrew in the latter half of the eighth century BCE;[9] the later version—the Septuagint—is the Greek translation of the Hebrew Bible, initiated some five hundred years later in Alexandria[10] by Jewish scribes, who placed the tree of knowledge of good and bad at the very beginning of creation to demonstrate the paramount importance of ethics in Judaism.

The "Late Date" Solution

Some exegetes have come up with the "late date" solution to explain why no mention is made of Eve and Adam in the rest of the Hebrew Bible. They attribute the omission to the late date of the Eden composition, supposedly written sometime between the Persian domination of Judea (fifth century BCE) and the Ptolemaic period (fourth century BCE).[11] This "late date" theory is rejected by William Schniedewind on the basis of biblical language and the fate of the northern tribes of Israel. Linguistic studies have noted distinct characteristics in the narrative language of the Torah/Pentateuch that are not found in such later works as Ezra–Nehemiah, Jubilees, or Ben Sira (fifth to second centuries BCE). The linguistic evidence based on the language and spirit of these later works[12] "precludes," for Schniedewind, "a very late dating of the composition of the Bible."[13] Moreover, unlike pre-exilic Israel, no mention is made of post-exilic Israel. The northern tribes, so prominent in the pre-exilic stories of Genesis, in the tribal history of Exodus, and in the traditions incorporated in Deuteronomy, are not mentioned in post-exilic Ezra–Nehemiah for good reason: the Assyrian army crushed the insurrection of Israel in 722 BCE, exiling the cultural, economic, and military elites of Israelite society. This expulsion rendered the northern tribes irrelevant, so that by the end of the seventh century BCE,[14] they were totally ignored. To argue, as Schniedewind does, that Judean scribes in the sixth century wrote detailed stories about Israelites who had disappeared from the stage of history more than a century earlier makes the "late date" solution indefensible.

The case against the "late date" composition of the Torah/Pentateuch is further supported by the despoliation prevailing in fifth-century Judah. Its decision to stop paying tribute to Babylonia in 586 BCE resulted in its devastation by the Babylonians. The temple in Jerusalem was destroyed, and Judah's military, economic, and cultural elites were exiled to Babylon. Though Judah was not entirely emptied of its inhabitants, so many were sent into exile that by the end of the fourth century BCE, the population of Jerusalem did not exceed fifteen hundred.[15] This chaotic situation forced the Levitical priesthood and singers to take up residence in the countryside, since an impoverished Jerusalem could no longer sustain them (Neh 13:10). Without the material resources necessary to underwrite the composition of the Torah/Pentateuch, "it is difficult to imagine," writes Schniedewind, "that there were the social conditions in antiquity that would encourage a great literary flourishing."[16]

Distortion

For the eighth-century prophets Isaiah and Hosea, Eve was above reproach, but by the second century CE, Eve represented all that was evil in the world. Carol Meyers attributes this change to the traditions handed down by the rabbinic sages and the church fathers about a millennium after the composition of Genesis 2–3.[17] These traditions, exerting an anti-feminist influence on gender roles and relationships, reflected the views of these religious functionaries on gender, sex, and sin. Because the rabbinic sages and the church fathers were held in such high esteem, their misogynistic commentaries on the Eden story assumed the dogmatic force of authority. The effect, observes Meyers, is that "we inevitably look at it through their interpretive eyes without realizing that translations and expositions of Genesis 2–3 may distort or misrepresent the meaning and function of the tale in its Israelite context."[18]

Just when these misrepresentations of the Eden story were accepted as authoritative is not known, but by the time the Hebrew Bible was translated into the Greek Septuagint, the denigration of women had become so accepted that Ben Sira could write in Ecclesiasticus (early second century BCE) that sin had its beginning with a woman, and because of her, everyone is destined to die (Sir 25:24).

Exonerating Eve

Though Eve and Adam choose to be progenitors of the human race, popular acceptance of the Eden story has relegated Eve's daughters to second-class citizenship in too many quarters of the globe. With second-class citizenship comes the loss of self-esteem. Despite the zealous effort by feminist exegetes to present Eve in a different light,[19] they have not succeeded in shaking off the general perception of a willfully disobedient Eve. This image still affects the treatment of women by the way it shapes the social attitudes people have as children. Whether the story is believed or not, writes Elaine Pagels, author of *Adam, Eve, and the Serpent*, "it's in you, a background perception."[20] Working subliminally in the minds of men, this perception of holding woman responsible for the world's sin and corruption is brought to the level of consciousness in a caricature of Eve in the Zondervan Manga Bible series.[21] Here she confides to the reader that she is able to break down Adam's resistance, because "girls can make guys do anything."[22] This cartoonish rendition is yet another instance of a long-standing practice, according to Rev. Rob Bell, the evangelical founding pastor of Mars Hill Bible Church, of using the Garden of Eden story to blame women "for everything that's wrong with the world and to keep them in their place."[23]

The Misreading of Divine Punishment

The idea of divine punishment is rooted in a fundamental misreading of the Hebrew text. Nowhere is eating the fruit forbidden. God simply warns Eve of what will happen to her physically after she eats the fertility-conferring fruit. She will experience the intense pain of delivery, not because of what she has done, but because childbirth is always accompanied by pain (chapter 12). Yet, despite the prospect of attendant pain and eventual death, Eve decides to bear a child, thereby rejecting the stagnation of Eden for its alternative—the creation of life.

The Search for Dual Meanings

In trying to make sense of the Hebrew text of Genesis 1–3, I found at times the "accepted" meaning of the Hebrew word to be unacceptable, compelling a search for alternative meanings of key Hebrew words. Unfortunately, the lexicons do not contain all the Hebrew words spoken in biblical times.[24] Omit the names in the Hebrew Bible, and its vocabulary shrinks to about three thousand words, whereas Egyptian and Akkadian dictionaries contain not less than fifteen thousand words. Indeed, observes W. F. Albright, it is "absurd for biblical scholars to insist that we must limit our vocabulary to Hebrew words found in standard Hebrew dictionaries."[25]

Complicating the search for dual meanings is the twenty-five percent that appear only once in the Hebrew Bible.[26] So, I turned to Rabbinic/Mishnaic Hebrew, the richest source for adding to one's knowledge of biblical Hebrew, since no wall of demarcation separated biblical from Rabbinic Hebrew in the developmental stages of the Hebrew language.[27] This treasure trove not only preserves ancient words that may or may not be confirmed in earlier documents,[28] but the pithy and precise phrasing of the vocabulary of everyday life also provides a rich earthiness,[29] generally absent in the translations of Hebrew Scripture.

Influence of Greek Literature

As with *The Drunkenness of Noah*, I found Homeric Greek concepts invaluable in studying biblical words relating to fertility, childbearing, and odors. That Homeric Greek biological concepts contribute to a more comprehensive understanding of biblical biology is supported by the many examples offered by Richard Broxton Onians. Additional parallels are found in John Pairman Brown's *Israel and Hellas*, a three-volume study of the religious, political, and cultural relationships between ancient Israel and Greece. Brown lists evidence from the texts "that the two societies were in touch at one or more removes" and that the texts witness "that the two societies were engaged in *parallel enterprises* with a *shared vocabulary of common nouns* [and a few verbs too]" (emphasis mine).[30]

These parallel structures, developed from the cultural entity formed by Crete and the coastal areas south of the city-state of Ugarit on the Syrian coast by the second millennium BCE, were fostered by the importation of mercenaries and people skilled in the arts, the establishment of trading stations, the international attraction of religious centers, and the mobility of religious personnel.[31] Ties between West Semitic and Greek cultures were further strengthened by the widespread use of the Semitic language throughout the area.[32] Indeed, Hebrew and Greek texts show that Israel and Greece lived in the same geopolitical world of states and rulers, sharing not only a vocabulary of common nouns, but also of proper names.[33]

Eve's Effect on Young Girls

Unlike Adam's reference to Eve as his "darling Rib" in Jeanne Steig's *The Old Testament Made Easy*, the conventional depiction of Eve is anything but innocuous for children. In a study of schoolchildren, ranging from five through eleven in age, young girls were particularly distressed by the conventional portrayal of Eve. To what degree this portrayal affected them is revealed by the number of girls who became "gender defectors" after being told that Eve disobeyed the divine commandment not to eat the fruit. Normally, children are expected to identify with a same-sex character, but not in the case of Eve. Nearly one-third of the girls rejected her as a flawed model, identifying instead with either Adam or God. Patently, these children did not want to identify with someone who is punished for disobedience. Telling this story without comment or judgment, writes Stuart Charmé, "is likely to elicit and reinforce in many children gender roles and gender identity that presuppose the inferiority and subordination of women."[34] A child's negative impression of Eve carried into adulthood is revealed in a woman's reaction to a sermon praising Eve's resourcefulness as benefiting the human race. After the service she told the feminist scholar delivering the sermon that she had lived with a sense of shame for bearing the name Eve, but, after hearing Eve extolled, she now could reclaim her name.[35]

Reassessing God

A reassessment of Eve leads to a reassessment of God. In the opinion of Katharina von Kellenbach, God opposes "independent thinking and decision-making and, instead, punishes maturity and self-determination."[36] In my rendition of the Garden of Eden story God does just the opposite. Benevolently, He treats Eve and Adam as adults, who accept the consequences of their independent thinking and decision-making. By clothing them with tunics and providing them with the means of sustenance after Eden, God expresses His admiration for the autonomous life they will lead as they embark into the unknown with dignity intact.

Narrative Technique

The account of the creation of the woman and man in Genesis 1 employs a literary technique known as "synoptic/resumptive."[37] The synoptic function, for Erich Kahler, is "to concentrate, to distil the essence out of phenomenality ... to see things in perspective and as wholes."[38] Thus, Genesis 1 is "synoptic" in cryptically distilling the essence of the phenomenon of creation of the universe and humanity, while Genesis 2–3 is "resumptive" in expanding upon Genesis 1 with flashback information about the creation of the woman and the man.[39] Connecting synoptic Genesis 1 with resumptive Genesis 2–3 is Genesis 2:4, the verse that introduces a detailed account of the creation of earth.[40]

Linking the synoptic with the resumptive in Genesis 1–3 are the dual names of God. In the creation account of Genesis 1, Umberto Cassuto regards *Elohim*, "God," as "a wholly transcendental Being, who abides in His own high sphere without contact with the creatures."[41] Conversely, the divine name *Yahweh*, "Lord," (KJV, JPS) in Genesis 2–3 denotes the God of Israel, who relates directly and personally with human beings and with nature.[42] By coupling the two divine names *Yahweh Elohim*, "Lord God," in Genesis 2–3, the narrator is saying in effect that *Yahweh*, the God of Israel, is to be identified with the transcendental *Elohim*, "God," as the creator of the universe.[43]

Contrasting Reproduction Stories

The apex of creation in Genesis 1 is the fashioning of the first woman and man, but their creation falls short of perfection. When told by God to "be fruitful and multiply" (Gen 1:28), they learn they have been created without reproductive ability. How Eve and Adam acquire the ability to become fertile and then to "multiply" is the overriding theme in the expansive, resumptive section of Genesis 2–3. Yet, even in the synoptic section of Genesis 1, the narrator asserts through his choice of words for "male" and "female" that propagation occurs only through sexual intercourse. This focus on the biology of reproduction is reflected in the Hebrew *zachar*, "male," derived from the verb *zachar*, "to prick, pierce,"[44] and *n'keivah*, "female," from the verb *nakav*, "to make a hole."[45] This emphasis on coital reproduction is expressed by Sisera's mother, who boasts of the "wombs" taken captive by her son (Judg 5:39).

Autochthonous Creation

This emphasis on sexual intercourse as the mode of propagation is a rejection of the Greek idea of autochthonous creation,[46] so prominently featured in the story of Deucalion and his wife Pyrrha, the sole survivors of the worldwide flood. Forewarned by his father Prometheus that everyone will perish in the impending deluge, Deucalion builds a wooden chest large enough for himself and his wife to ride out the flood. When the waters finally recede, they are so overcome by the desolation of the land that they ask the goddess Themis what they can do to resuscitate humanity. The goddess advises them to cover their heads and toss the bones of their "great mother" behind them. At first perplexed by these instructions, Deucalion and Pyrrha finally figure out that their great mother is earth and that stones are her bones.[47] Following the advice of the goddess, they toss the stones, which slowly soften and assume human shapes. "The moist and earthen part of the stones," writes Ovid, "turned into flesh, the part that was solid and unbendable changed to bones … the stones cast behind him by Deucalion took on the likeness of men, those thrown by Pyrrha became women."[48]

From Stones to Bones

A story of stones transformed into people may well have been known to John the Baptist, because he speaks of God creating new children of Abraham out of stone (Matthew 3:9). The narrator of the Eden story also must have known of such an account, because he describes Adam as created out of *afar*, which should be translated as "stone," not "dust" (Gen

2:7). While the Hebrew Bible is replete with examples of *afar* as "dust,"[49] it does not mean, cautions Peter Ackroyd, "that in other passages it can automatically be understood in the same way."[50] One such passage is Genesis 2:7, where *afar* as fine, dry, particulate matter is rejected by E. A. Speiser as "inappropriate."[51] He prefers "clods,"[52] which he defines as "lumps of earth, soil, dirt."[53] Speiser pictures Adam as molded into a human being from the more substantive clod of earth, rather than from dry, particulate matter. Yet a clod of earth falls short, because it does not provide the hardness needed for fashioning the skeleton of a human being. That solidity is achieved when *afar* is understood as "stone," as illustrated in passages from Genesis and Job.

Afar is used as "stone" in the story of Isaac seeking refuge in Philistine territory from the drought that devastated the land during Abraham's time (Gen 26:12–15). Isaac and his extended family not only are granted refuge by the Philistines, but also are permitted to farm the same area and to use the wells dug by Abraham. Some Philistines, envious of Isaac's large flocks and bountiful harvest, maliciously stop up Abraham's wells with *afar*, translated here as "earth," (JPS, NJPS). But *afar* has to mean "stones" when read in the context of the military strategy adopted by the Israelites against the Moabites: "… stop up every spring, and ruin every fertile plot with stones" (2 Kgs 3:19). Stones, littering the landscape everywhere, could easily have been scooped up for damming the springs and preventing cultivation of the land. The Philistines, knowing of such a strategy, would have stopped up Isaac's wells with *afar*, here understood as the collective for "stones." Stopping up the well with stones would have been done far quicker than digging up hard, sun-baked chunks of dirt for dumping down a well shaft.

Additional support for translating *afar* as "stone" is found in Job 28:2, which speaks of iron ore that is mined and copper that is melted. Marvin Pope translates this verse as: "Iron is taken from the dust/Copper is melted from stone."[54] In his notes, however, Pope speaks of iron as derived from terrestrial ore, a type of mineral rock mentioned in Deuteronomy 8:9 in reference to iron. The poet's synonymous parallelism[55] is readily perceived with *afar* as "stone, rock."

"Bone of My Bone ..."

The fashioning of Eve from a stone throws new light on the creation of Adam. After God forms Eve from Adam's rib, He presents her to Adam, who then exclaims: "'This one at last is bone of my bones and flesh of my flesh'" (Gen 2:23, NJPS). Adam's acknowledgment of Eve as his exact counterpart means that he too is created of bone and flesh. Since Adam has no predecessor to provide a rib, God makes do with the one substance that is hard enough and strong enough for shaping Adam's skeleton: *afar*, "stone." But this *afar* is not just stone; rather it is *min ha-adamah*, "from/in the earth." Far from being a gratuitous piece of information, the phrase "from/in the earth" is to be understood as "dirt, earth" imbedded in the stone. Like Ovid's moist and earthen part of the stone, this is the raw material that is transformed into the flesh that fills out Adam's frame; in like manner, the flesh adhering to Adam's rib becomes the flesh that fills out Eve's frame. Such duplication allows Adam to declare that Eve is his exact counterpart.

Divine Solicitude

In Genesis 2–3 God shows His concern for the future welfare of Eve and Adam by creating new sources of food to supplement the sixth day's creation of *b'heimah*, "livestock (herbivores)" and *chaiyat haarets*, the carnivorous, undomesticated "beast of the earth" (Gen 1:24–25). Since the carnivorous beasts are restricted to a vegetarian diet (Gen 1:30)—death has not yet been introduced—they are reduced to munching on carrots instead of lamb bones.

To provide Eve and Adam with another source of food, God, in Genesis 2, creates the game animal *chaiyat hasadeh*, "beast of the field," such as the gazelle, oryx, and ibex; these animals inhabit the semiarid *sadeh*, "field," a technical term for that part of the countryside abounding in game. Esau, a hunter, is described as an *ish hasadeh*, "a man of the field" (Gen 25:27), who fulfills Isaac's deathbed request that he take bow and quiver to hunt for venison in the "field" (Gen 27:3).

Along with "the fowl of the air" and "every beast of the field" (Gen 2:20, JPS) to be named by Adam, the narrator includes the *b'heimah*, "cattle/livestock," created on the sixth day (Gen 1:24–25). The birds in Genesis 1, created on the fifth day, are not classified as game. Compared with game fowl, they move in markedly different flight patterns. The birds "fly above the earth in the open firmament of heaven" (Gen 1:20, JPS). The firmament, visualized as a dome or vault (Gen 1:20, NEB), is so high that people appear as "grasshoppers" to God as He looks down from the vaulted heavens.[56] So, birds flying across this expanse of open sky would appear as tiny objects to the person observing their flight, too high to be caught in snares. But this would not be true for low-flying "fowl of the air," such as the desert partridge and sandgrouse.[57] Quails, at some point toward the end of their migratory route, would also fit into this category, as in the story of quails driven off course by high winds and falling exhausted into the Sinaitic camp of the fleeing Hebrews (Exod 16:13, Num 11:31–32).

The picture of quails falling from the sky is not a figment of the narrator's imagination. According to Major C. S. Jarvis, the British Governor of Sinai in the 1930s, large flocks of these birds from Russia, Romania, and Hungary would migrate in the fall to North Africa, and then on to Sinai and Egypt, returning to Europe in the spring. Toward the end of their long flight across the Mediterranean, many would fall exhausted to the ground. Anticipating their migration, the Bedouin of northern Sinai facilitated their capture by stringing up big trammel nets along the seashore to snare the fowl in droves as they flew low above the shore. [58]

After leaving Eden, Eve and Adam find the countryside suitable for farming grains, fruits, and vegetables; the uncultivated land ready for grazing livestock; and the arid desert ideal for snaring fowl and hunting the gazelle and ibex.[59]

The stage is now set for the drama of Eden to unfold.

1.
EYES AND FERTILITY: THE PHYSIOLOGICAL CONNECTION

> When the woman saw that the tree was good for eating and was a delight to the eyes, and that the tree was desirable as a source of wisdom, she took of its fruit and ate; and she gave some to her husband also, and he ate. Then the eyes of both of them were opened and they perceived that they were naked … (Gen 3:6–7, NJPS).

Objections to a Metaphor

"Then the eyes of both of them were opened …"

Is Scripture saying that Eve and Adam have been walking around the garden with their eyes closed before eating the fruit of the Tree of Knowledge of Good and Bad? Not at all, for the text clearly states that Eve "saw that the tree was good for eating and a delight to the eyes" *before* eating the fruit (Gen 3:6), and that Adam was able to distinguish between the different forms of animal life *before* eating the fruit (Gen 2:20).

Then is Scripture being inconsistent here? No, assert scholars, for "opening of the eyes" is not to be taken literally. It is a metaphor, signifying the falling away of the veil of ignorance. Upon eating the fruit, Eve and Adam become open to new sources of knowledge previously hidden from them.[60]

But if "opening of the eyes" is a metaphor, that would mean the *nachash*, commonly assumed to be a snake, is speaking metaphorically when it says to Eve: "'You are not going to die. God knows that as soon as you eat of it, your eyes will be opened and you will be like divine beings[61] who know good and bad'" (Gen 3:4–5, NJPS). Since figurative language is never attributed to a non human in the Hebrew Bible, the *nachash* must be speaking literally when it predicts what will happen if Eve eats the fruit. Underscoring the literal meaning of the words of the nachash is the verb *pakach*, "to open," a word primarily used to express the opening of one's eyes after the removal of an ophthalmic blockage. But how does the nachash know about ophthalmic blockages, since nothing in the narrative even hints that Eve and Adam have a vision problem? The answer lies with the fruit: upon eating the fruit, the nachash acquires a particular property relating to sight.

In dealing with the nachash, Eve reveals she is not a naïve babe in the woods. She does not ask the creature to explain the meaning of "divine beings," "good and bad," and "death," because she is already familiar with these terms. If she were not, she would have asked for clarification with the same purposefulness she exhibits when she sets the nachash straight about God's directive regarding the trees (Gen 3:1–2). That Eve, as well as Adam, would know about divine beings, though the text says nothing more about them, or about death—a phenomenon yet to be introduced into the story—is to be explained by the concept of *instant maturation*.

Instant Maturation

Instant maturation is manifest in Hesiod's account of the birth of Apollo.[62] The goddess Delos, having given permission to pregnant Leto to give birth on her rocky island of Delos, fears that Apollo, *at birth*, will act haughtily, "scorning" her rocky island as soon as he sees the light of the sun (III, 65–75).[63] Her fear is justified, for at birth, Apollo not only scorns the rocky island, but also exhibits another earmark of immediate maturation when he declares that the lyre and the curved bow will ever be dear to him, as he begins to walk "the wide-pathed earth" (III, 125–135) to the amazement of the attending goddesses.[64]

Rabbinic exegetes acknowledged the instant maturation of Eve, as well as Adam, in *Genesis Rabbah*, a collection of Jewish homiletical interpretations on the book of Genesis compiled at the end of the fourth and the beginning of the fifth century. Thus, Rabbi Joshua, son of Rabbi Nehemiah, commenting on the words "male and female He created them" (Gen 1:27), says that God created in Adam four traits applicable to beings of the upper world: "he stands up straight like ministering angels, he speaks as do ministering angels, he has the power of understanding as do ministering angels, and he sees as do ministering angels."[65] Rabbi Judah bar Simon, expounding on "[The Lord God formed man] of dust [from the ground]" (Gen 2:7), declares that Adam was created "a fully formed young man." Rabbi Eleazar bar Simeon adds that Eve too was created "fully formed,"[66] and Rabbi Yochanan estimates that "Adam and Eve were created at the age of twenty years."[67]

The nachash can assure Eve she is not going to die from eating the fruit, because it has eaten the fruit and is still alive to tell the tale! What presumably persuades Eve to accept this eyewitness account is the physical reaction of the nachash to the fruit. The creature stands before her in a state of intense sexual arousal, its "opened"[68] eyes attesting to the procreativity of the fruit. A complete analysis of this transformation is presented in chapter 7, "The Lustful Centaur," but for now it is enough to acknowledge that the creature is not a snake, but an ithyphallic man-horse[69] primed to engage in coitus with Eve after she is eroticized by the fruit.[70]

That the nachash acquired the ability to procreate upon eating the fruit is confirmed when God tells the nachash that He will put enmity between it and Eve, and between its offspring and hers (Gen 3:15). Since nowhere does the Eden narrative speak of the procreativity of the nachash, it is to be concluded from the reference to its offspring that the nachash becomes fertile by eating the fruit of the tree in the middle of the garden.

The Technical Meaning of "Opened"

In one respect, the Hebrew verb *pakach* corresponds to the Homeric Greek conception of sight, which has "no one verb," according to Bruno Snell, "to refer to the function of sight as such, but that there were several verbs each designating a specific type of vision."[71] Apparently *pakach*, "to ophthalmically open the eyes," is the Hebrew equivalent to the Greek conception of sight, in that it is restricted to that one specific situation where life can either be endangered or lost.[72]

In the case of Hagar and her son Ishmael, *pakach* underscores their dire plight. Driven off into the desert wilderness, they become so dehydrated that Hagar moves Ishmael under a shrub to avoid witnessing his death throes. Then God "opens" (*pakach*) her eyes to a well; she sees it, draws water, and gives it to her son. Their lives are spared (Gen 21:8–21). In this instance, "opening the eyes" indicates that Hagar, whose vision has been impaired by her life-threatening ordeal, now has recovered her vision completely.

In the episode where Elisha and his servant find themselves surrounded by soldiers of the King of Aram (2 Kgs 6:8–17), the terrified servant runs to him, certain that neither he nor his master can escape death, whereupon Elisha prays that God would *pakach*, "open," the eyes of his servant to the horses and chariots of fire sent to prevent their capture. The servant, no longer hindered by an ocular impediment, is reassured by the sight of the chariots of fire that he need not fear the soldiers of Aram.

Even more striking is the use of *pakach* in the revival of the lifeless son of the Shunammite woman. To restore life to the child, Elisha stretches out upon this lifeless body, his mouth, eyes, and hands upon the mouth, eyes, and hands of the child. In mouth-to-mouth breathing, Elisha transfers his *nefesh*, "stuff of consciousness," to restore consciousness to the child. Then, placing his hands upon the hands of the boy, Elisha transfers strength to the child; and through eye-to-eye contact, he breathes out rays of light from his eyes to restore sight to the child by penetrating death's band of mist or cloud. The flesh of the child becomes warm, his eyes "open" (*pakach*), and life is restored (2 Kgs 4:8–37). Here Elisha's eyes emit rays of light much like Plato's "inner fire" that "flashes forth like lightning"[73] and is "made to flow through the eyes in a stream smooth and dense."[74]

Tangible Death

Though Eve and Adam are in no immediate danger of dying, the use of *pakach* signifies an ophthalmic obstruction similar to that manifested by the dying Hagar, whose vision is obstructed by something tangible, like darkness in the form of a cloud, or mist that veils the eyes in death or imminent death, much like the black cloud of grief covering Laertes.[75] In Scripture, death, or the prospect of death, is associated with a covering or veil, as when the servants of King Ahasuerus cover Haman's face (Esther 7:8) to denote death's cover of darkness that will soon envelop the head of the doomed vizier,[76] or the "shadow of death"—the darkness of approaching death—that will cover Job's eyes and head (Job 16:16).[77]

The palpability of death is also manifest in the darkness of the ninth plague: "And the Lord said unto Moses: 'Stretch out thy hand toward heaven, that there may be darkness over the land of Egypt, even darkness which may be felt'" (Exod 10:21, JPS). Tellingly, the plague of darkness precedes the tenth plague—the slaying of the Egyptian firstborn. Thus, palpable darkness, "a darkness which may be felt," becomes the harbinger of approaching death. In contrast, the light in the dwellings of the Hebrew slaves (Exod 10:23) indicates that they, unlike the Egyptian firstborn, are not marked for death.

The act of seeing in the aforementioned episodes involves an actual cutting or breaking through the band of darkness obstructing full vision. This biblical concept of a force pushing aside and cutting through all impediments to sight is retained in rabbinic Hebrew, which defines *pakach* as "opening up a heap of debris."[78] Unlike Hagar and the son of the Shunammite woman, however, Eve and Adam need no outside force to break through this "heap of debris" brought on by death or imminent death, since death has yet to be introduced into the story. Rather their ocular impediment stems from their being created without *procreative fluid.*

This deficiency, manifest in Hesiod as dryness,[79] renders them *less than fully alive.* Ancient Israelites must have known either from personal experience or from aging family members of an obstruction found in the pupil of the glaucomatous eye. Premodern medicine described this disease as the desiccation of vision, a condition when eyes "dry up, become stone."[80] For Eve and Adam to attain full vision, they must counteract the dryness of their eyes with the generative fluid found in the head.

The Head as the Seat of Procreation

Counteracting dryness of the eyes with generative fluid was anything but bizarre[81] for the Homeric Greeks, who equated death with a parched and desiccated body resulting from the depletion of a person's life-fluid. [82] This life-fluid, originating in the spinal marrow and cerebral tissue and stored in the head,[83] is the fluid of procreation, as evidenced by the growth of a person's hair. Judging by the Tantras of Bengal and the headhunting Iban of Sarawak, Greeks were not unique in believing generative fluid is stored in the head.[84] In a ritual splitting of a trophy head by the Iban god of war, semen pours forth, which, when sown, grows into a human crop.[85] The headhunters of Sarawak, knowing nothing of ancient Greek culture, performed a ritual that recalls not only the Homeric belief in the head as a source of semen, but also the feat of Cadmus, who sowed dragon's teeth on the plain of Boeotia.

Homeric Greeks reasoned that moisture and wetness of the eyes reflect the procreative fluid stored in the head, and that tears are the seed, the *aion,* or liquid, in the body that is one with the cerebrospinal fluid.[86] Thus, tears melting the cheeks of Penelope, as she listens to the disguised Odysseus, represent the life that fills and forms her flesh;[87] for the region around her eyes, being part of the head, reflects an abundance of seed.[88] Sexual love then is a process of liquefying or flowing at the eyes, characterized as *hygros*, the swimming eyes of sexual passion,[89] while the gravely ill person, whose liquid *aion* "melts" through sweating, is depicted as dried up.[90] In short, youth's wetness of eyes and softness of flesh connotes an ample store of the seed of sexual potency.

Notably, halfway around the globe and roughly three thousand years later, the whaling community of Nantucket, the tiny island about twenty-five miles off southeastern Massachusetts, also located the procreative fluid of the sperm whale in the head. Nantucket, the whaling capital of the world during the late eighteenth and early nineteenth centuries, concentrated on hunting the sperm whale, because, writes Nathaniel Philbrick, its block head "contained a vast reservoir of even better oil, called spermaceti … It was spermaceti's resemblance to seminal fluid that gave rise to the sperm whale's name."[91]

Leah's Wet Eyes

The Hebrew narrator, conversant with the Semitic equivalent of Greek *aion*, associates Leah's eyes with the wetness of sexuality. After her sister Rachel is portrayed as "shapely and beautiful" (Gen 29:17, NJPS), the narrator seemingly exhausts his store of adjectives, because nothing is said about Leah's face or figure. He does, however, describe her eyes as *rakot*, "weak" or "dull," seemingly a condition associated with some ophthalmic condition. An alternative translation of "tender, soft" is not any better, considering how Rachel is commended for her figure and appearance. This picture of Leah as a listless, dull-eyed woman, who would have worn glasses with thick lenses had the practice of ophthalmology flourished in ancient times, changes once *rakot* is read in the context of the story. Not poor Leah, but *blessed* Leah; for *rakot* gives an immediate reading of her store of fertility: Leah is brimming with fecundity!

In a society that believes a barren woman to be cursed, Leah's eyes reveal her capacity to be a mother many times over. The dual meaning of *rakot* as "soft" and "wet"—in rabbinic Hebrew "soft (liquid) juice," as contrasted with "thick (jelly-like) juice"—expresses the idea of flowing liquid juice.[92] With the focus on the wetness of Leah's eyes, the narrator presents a vivid picture of her sexual potency that will be demonstrated many times over with her husband Jacob.

The connection between fertility and the wetness of the eyes also is found in the story of Judah and his daughter-in-law Tamar, who is left childless by the death of Er, the oldest of Judah's three sons (Gen 38: 6–7). In compliance with the law of levirate marriage (Deut 25:5–10), Tamar is given in marriage to Onan, Judah's second son, so that their first-born child would be considered the child of his deceased brother Er. But Onan dies after refraining from impregnating Tamar. At this point, Judah advises Tamar to live in her father's house until Shelah, his youngest son, is old enough for marriage. However, when Shelah reaches the appropriate age, Judah reneges on his promise to Tamar, fearful his son will suffer the same fate as his brothers. Tamar, "single-minded, fearless, and totally self-confident,"[93] learns that Judah, now a widower, will be joining his sheepshearers at Timnah. Determined to bear a child of the stock of Judah, she dresses as a harlot, covers her face with a veil, and waits by the entrance of the oasis Enaim, translated as "Two Springs,"[94] which is on the way to Timnah. Judah, stopping to refresh himself at the oasis, is seduced by Tamar into having sex with her. Unrecognizable in her harlot's attire, she is impregnated by Judah and months later she gives birth to twin boys, one of whom becomes the ancestral father of David.

The belief that the water of Enaim fosters impregnation is supported by its alternative Hebrew meaning of "eyes." The combination of these two translations—"Two Springs and "Eyes"—accentuates the physiological fact that wetness (water) of the eyes signifies fertility.[95] Presumably, the oasis of "Two Springs/Eyes" was frequented by barren women seeking to acquire the "wet eyes" of fecundity by drinking its water. Obviously, Tamar determined the oasis to be the ideal place for the seduction of Judah. That other springs were believed to contain similar properties is to be concluded from the negative effects of the Jericho spring, where pregnant women suffer miscarriages after drinking its water. When Elisha hears of the plight of these women, he empties a flask of salt into its source (2 Kings 2: 19–22) to restore the spring to its former, pregnancy-enhancing state.[96]

The Enfeebling Effect of Blindness

Eve's eyes, before they are "opened," may have appeared dull or darkened, but her condition is in no way comparable to that of the blinded Samson, rendered powerless when his hair is cut (Judg 16:20–25). His ophthalmic condition is to be attributed to a single cause: the absence of procreative fluid in the head. Blinded by his captors, Samson is brought to Gaza, where he is bound with bronze shackles and set in the prison house to "grind" (Judg 16:21, JPS). Significantly, his hair does not have to be cut again, because his strength never returns to its original state after he is blinded by the Philistines, who are intent on drying up his cranial procreative fluid.[97]

Working on the premise that darkness precipitates a drought-like condition by causing greenery to die after being cut off from sunlight, the Philistines deprive Samson of his strength by setting up the necessary condition for internal "drought": the pitch-darkness of sightlessness. Jeremiah knows of this relationship between darkness and drought when he describes the desert through which God led the people as "a dry and pitch-dark land" (Jer 2:6).[98] The same idea is present in the etymological relationship between *erev*, "evening, dusk," and *aravah*, "a dry, waterless region."[99] A permanent darkening of the eyes, unlike the "liquid eyes" of generative fluid, results in the same deprivation of moisture as that suffered by prisoners exposed to the "arid" condition of a pitch-black dungeon. Isaiah compares the release of these prisoners into the sunlight as opening (*pakach*) the eyes of the blind (Isa 42:7).

The same relationship between blindness and dryness is expressed in the account of the revolt of Korah, Dathan, and Abiram against Moses. Painfully aware that they are dying a slow death in the desert, they scornfully reject Moses's summons for a meeting by asking: "... wilt thou put out the eyes of these men?" (Num 16:14, JPS). Though the verbal root of *nakar*, "to put out the eyes, to blind," is also used in the Samson story, nowhere in the account of the revolt against Moses is mention made of people being blinded. Rather, this "blindness" is the darkness resulting from dryness. Weakened, dried up, and devoid of seminal fluid, Dathan and Abiram charge Moses with "blinding" them by leading them into a desert, devoid of greenery or moisture.

As for Moses at the time of his death, "his eye had not become dim, nor was his *lach* dried up."[100] With *lach* as seminal fluid that translates into bodily vigor,[101] Moses owes the brightness of his eye to the seminal fluid that connects directly to the eye from the head. The dimming of Moses's eye would have signaled a loss of sexual potency, and a dimming of his eye to the point of blindness would have been taken as the total absence of seminal fluid. The Psalmist, equating loss of vision with loss of strength,[102] declares: "… my strength has left me, and the light of my eyes, it too has gone" (Psa 38:11).

The location of seminal fluid in the head becomes the focal point of David's execration of Joab. To impair the procreative capacity of Joab and his descendants for treacherously murdering Abner,[103] David directs his malediction specifically against their heads so that subsequent offspring will disgrace the memory of the virile Joab with leprosy, continuous genital discharge, poor performance on the battlefield, and a failure to garner food. In his diatribe against Joab and his household, David contrasts himself with Joab and his brother Abishai: "But I am this day a moist and anointed king, while these men, the sons of Zeruiah, are drier than I; the Lord will avenge their evil" (2 Sam 3:39). David, referring to himself as "wet/moist" and "anointed," ascribes his moisture to sexual potency, while Joab and Abishai, hard and dry as stubble, lack such potency. As the divinely anointed agent made powerful by a full supply of seminal fluid, David will be able to deal with the sons of Zeruiah, whose dried-up store of seminal fluid renders them impotent and weak.

Strength and Seminal Glistening

Glistening eyes, indicative of one's store of procreative fluid, is central to the story of Jonathan, who, unaware his father forbade his troops from eating until evening, dips the end of his spear into a honeycomb and puts it to his mouth, causing his eyes to brighten (1 Sam 14:27). When told that Saul has put a curse upon anyone disobeying his order, Jonathan remonstrates: "... see, I pray you, how mine eyes are brightened, because I tasted a little of this honey" (1 Sam 14:29, JPS). Jonathan is saying in effect that the brightness of a warrior's eyes reflects strength-bestowing seminal fluid, whereas a darkened eye signifies so serious a depletion of seminal fluid that the warrior has no strength to triumph in battle. In Jonathan's case, his brightened eyes connote a replenished seminal potency that infuses him with the vigor to engage the Philistines.

The opening of the pupil of the eye, ocular brightening, and an abundant supply of seminal fluid come together when pupils dilate and the eye-surface glistens during human sexual arousal. Kinsey and his co-authors report that at the moment of orgasm, as observed by the sexual partner, the eyes of the sexually aroused person may acquire a distinctive glare that is associated with a dilation of the pupils of the eyes, an unfocused staring, and a glistening of the eyes due to increased lachrymal secretion.[104] John Updike describes just such a physical reaction in writing of a woman engaged in coitus: "Her dull blue eyes when she was making love, and a minute later, became as bright and dark as wet ink. Then they faded back . . . ."[105]

The correlation between pupil size of the eye and sexual stimulus is to be seen in a series of experiments that show men's pupils dilating more at the sight of a female pinup and women's pupils dilating more in response to a male pinup. To learn if pupil size enhances attractiveness, investigators then touched up the slides of two women from a series of photos, making one woman's pupils extra large, and the other woman's pupils extra small. The response to the picture of the woman with the enlarged pupils was more than twice as strong as the response to the woman with the small pupils, even though most of the men believed the photos to be identical. While some did not notice any difference in pupil size between the two women, they nevertheless observed that one was "more feminine," "prettier," or "softer."[106]

Viagra, a medication for sexual dysfunction, affected the pupil size of one user, who reported his eyes "grew bigger" after taking the prescribed dosage. The Pfizer Labs product information on Viagra confirms that cases of mydriasis—excessive dilation of the pupil of the eye—were reported from among the more than three thousand men tested.[107] Clearly, the Viagra participant and the Hebrew narrator attest to the ocular phenomenon of eyes "opening" or "growing bigger" in response to sexual stimulus. The Israelite woman, millennia before the advent of experimental psychology, knew she could turn a man on by painting her eyes to make them look larger and more brilliant.[108] And Jeremiah, aware of the erotic effect a woman with eyeliner can have upon a man, compares Jerusalem to a seductress, who decks herself with golden ornaments and enlarges her eyes with paint (Jer 4:30).

The Creation of Adam

The pupil of the eye and Elisha's act of resuscitation provide the key to Adam's creation. It will be recalled that just as Elisha restores consciousness (*nefesh*) to the Shunammite boy with his breath, so too God makes Adam a conscious human being, a *nefesh chaiyah*, "a living soul,"[109] by blowing the breath of life into his nostrils. However, the comparison stops here. While Elisha's contact with the hands and eyes of the boy allows him to transmit osmotically the qualities attributed to his procreative capacity of softness, vigor, and moisture, not so with Adam.[110] Adam's eyes are not fully "open," because his body at the time of creation does not produce the procreative fluid that makes for softness and moisture. Only when Adam is endowed with procreative fluid will the pupils of his eyes contribute to their "opening."

The Pupil as Sluice Gate

The Hebrew for "orifice of the eye"[111] or "opening" reveals that the pupil of the eye serves as a sluice gate. This identification of the pupil of the eye with a sluice gate is found in Ecclesiastes 12:3, where the Hebrew word *arubah*, "window" or "pupil" of the eye, also means "sluice" or "channel."[112] (Aramaic *bavitah* means both "pupil of the eye" and "gutter.")[113] The idea of sluices or channels leading to the eyes as part of the human vascular system must have come from the Egyptians, who laid the foundations of medical science more than fifty centuries ago.[114]

The Egyptians, reputed for their extensive medical skill in classical times,[115] acquired their knowledge of anatomy and physiology from their custom of embalming the dead, a procedure that necessitated the removal and handling of the viscera.[116] Over one hundred anatomical terms testify to the ability of the Egyptians to differentiate and name the body's many organs and organic structures. Though Egyptian knowledge of the nervous, muscular, and vascular systems did not compare with their knowledge of anatomy, their knowledge of nerves, muscles, arteries, and veins, nevertheless was considerable.[117] The Egyptians conceived a vascular structure consisting of a single system of branching cables, radiating from the heart and forming a second rallying point around the anus.[118] With the heart as the hub, the vessels carried blood, air, urine, feces, semen, tears, and mucus, depending on where they went. Believing internal decay to be a source of disease, the Egyptians visualized at least four of the twelve vessels leading directly to the anus to disgorge the deadly load of decayed material.[119] The biblical narrator integrated this Egyptian conception of the vascular system as a system of canals or "sewers" into his construct of the human body.

The Greeks later refined and supplemented Egyptian medical knowledge. Indeed, the investigations of the physiology of the nervous system by Galen of Pergamon (129—c. 200 CE) and his experiments on the spinal cord were not improved upon until the nineteenth century.[120] His painstaking research into the structure of the eyeball may explain why the ancients thought seminal fluid to be present in the eye. In dissecting the eyeball,

Galen ruptured the remaining stratum of the cornea, behind which flowed a colorless liquid that in the eyes of living animals resembled the fluid contained in eggs.[121] Since resemblance to an egg would have been associated with fertility, the Greeks concluded that the liquid in the human eye was a measure of the sap of fertility in that person. Corroborating this theory was Galen's discovery that in the sensory nerves extending to the eyes from the brain were channels through which the luminous psychic pneuma traveled to the eyes to give them their radiance and brightness.[122]

Assimilating the concepts of the vascular system then current in his east Mediterranean world, the biblical narrator selected *pakach* ("to open" the eyes) to denote how procreative fluid, coursing through the conduits of the human vascular system, bursts through the blockage of the sensory nerves leading to the eyes.[123] The "opened" eyes of Eve and Adam now testify to the potency they acquired from eating the fruit.

So, the nachash in the garden is right: Eve and Adam are now brimming with the fluid of life. How extraordinary is the fig!

2.
THE FIG TREE

Fig Leaves and Fertility

Eve and Adam eat the fruit of the fig tree, and then they sew fig leaves together to make themselves girdles (Gen 3:7), which may have been like girdles depicted on the monuments of Egypt and Sumer: a cord tied several times around the loins, with two small pieces of cloth attached in the front to cover the genitals.[124] Supposedly, Eve and Adam use fig leaves to shield their genitals from each other's gaze; however, the narrator says nothing about them shamefully walking about naked. If shame were the reason for covering one's genitals, banana leaves would have done a far better job. No, Eve and Adam cover their genitals with the leaves of the fig tree—self-fertile, not requiring pollination—[125] to maintain their newly acquired procreative power at full strength.

In ancient times, the fig tree was renowned for its reproductive power: "The tree bears its fruit, the fig tree and the vine exhibit their procreative power" (Joel 2:22).[126] This procreative power, attributed to the fruit of the fig tree, extended even to its leaves. Among the Baganda and the Kikuyu of Kenya, a barren wife would sew herself an apron of fig leaves from a sacred fig tree so that the leaves from a tree with an inexhaustible supply of fertility would transfer seed-conferring power directly to the organs they touch.[127] This practice of Kenyan tribal women most likely replicated an ancient custom from the Fertile Crescent, the locale of the Garden of Eden story. So, Eve and Adam give themselves an extra charge of potency by covering their genitals with fig leaves. Their desire to become parents, not the avoidance of shame, impels the first woman and man to dress in the haute couture of Eden.

The Potency of the Trunk

As potent as is the fig leaf, even more so is the trunk. Yet, the potency of the trunk seemingly is not even alluded to in Eve's repetition of God's warning: "It is only about the fruit of the tree in the middle of the garden that God said: 'You shall not eat of it or touch it, lest you die'" (Gen 3:3, NJPS). "It" generally is understood to refer to the fruit of the tree; however, one rabbinic tradition speaks of "it" as referring to the trunk.[128] The perceptiveness of this rabbinic observation may be gauged by the two related meanings of the Hebrew word *naga*, "to touch." In the episode of Sarah and Abimelech, king of the Philistines, *naga*, "to touch," has nothing to do with sensory perception when God informs the king in a dream that the woman taken into his harem is really Abraham's wife and that he is not to commit the sin of "touching" her (Gen 20:6). In this context, *naga*, "to touch," means "to engage in coitus." Why else would Sarah be brought into the harem, if not to fill the same sexual role as the other women? Similarly, *naga* is used in the episode where Rebecca is palmed off as Isaac's sister (Gen 26:11). Like the Latin verb *tangit*, "touches" or "pricks,"[129] *naga* means "to prick" or "to engage in sexual intercourse," as when Abimelech warns the populace to refrain from sexually molesting (*naga*) Rebecca or Isaac upon pain of death. Isaac is included in the interdiction to prevent his being sexually assaulted by Abimelech's men for deceiving them about his "sister."

With *naga* as "to prick" in Genesis 3:3, God cautions Eve and Adam against pricking the tree for its sap or "semen," which then would be used to increase the production of their own procreative fluid. That trees in the ancient east Mediterranean world were believed to produce semen is to be inferred from Aristotle's observation that willow and poplar trees are examples of living things that "actually produce no semen at all" (*Animals* 1.18.726a6). Not only was the human sap of generation considered to be the counterpart of the sap of plants,[130] but also certain juices of trees were called tears—tears of amber, tears of balsam, tears of resin—[131] reflecting the Homeric belief that tears were regarded as seed. Little wonder, then, that Eve and Adam are drawn to a tree that not only exudes this sap, but also produces leaves for recharging one's sexual organs.

The Fig Tree in the Ancient World

The fig tree, described by Theophrastus as "very full of sap" (*Plants* 4.2.2)[132] was prized for the medicinal qualities of its milky white sap, which causes milk to curdle (which it does) and blood to clot.[133] In the *Iliad*, the white milk of the fig tree is spread upon the spear wound of Ares to stem the flow of blood (5.902–3). Though the clotting quality of this sap has yet to be proved, the medicinal properties of fig tree juice were accepted as fact throughout antiquity. Indeed, so copious can be its exudation that some species have been used for the production of rubber.[134] Eve and Adam, knowing of the procreative power in the fig leaf and trunk, could have increased their store of procreative fluid by tapping the trunk of the fig tree for the milky sap that resembles human procreative fluid.

Just how Eve and Adam would use this milky sap is suggested by a word in Akkadian that not only means "to touch," but also means "to stroke, rub, smear, anoint."[135] Smearing this milky-white latex upon one's sexual organs was believed to stimulate a similar flow of sap in one's body—a line of thought that reflects the dominant medical opinion of the classical world. Pliny, who speaks of certain plants containing properties that determine the conception of one sex or the other, explains how this works. Eating the lower part of the stem of the satyrion promotes the conception of a male child, while the upper part of the stem promotes a female.[136] In addition to eating the plant or drinking its juice, a woman applies a potion made of the leaves of the female plant of the linozostis to her genital area to assure conception of a female, while a male is engendered by applying a potion made of the leaves of the male plant to the penis.[137] In addition, smearing the body with resin from a terebinth tree and goose grease for two days results in male offspring, provided that intercourse takes place the next day.[138] That sap of the terebinth is one of the two essential ingredients for sex determination supports the idea that the milky-white latex of the fig tree enhances procreation.

The Divine Warning Against Touching

God says nothing to Adam about not "touching/pricking" the tree. Assigned "to till and tend" the garden (Gen 2:15, NJPS), Adam is told he may eat the fruit of every tree in the garden except the fruit of a certain tree in the midst of the garden. This omission has caused some scholars to conclude that Eve, to her shame or credit, is responsible for expanding upon God's words. Rabbinic sages, attributing to Eve a penchant for exaggeration,[139] reasoned that she would not have been tempted to eat the fruit had she not added to God's words. But, as "the more intelligent one, the more aggressive one and the one with the greater sensibilities,"[140] observes Phyllis Trible, she interprets God's warning to mean that they are not even to "touch" it.

Before Eve is to be commended for her sagacity or castigated for her embellishment, it seems more likely that responsibility for this supposed embellishment lies with the storyteller to keep the attention of his audience. In some episodes in Genesis the narrator later inserts details of earlier incidents to heighten the dramatic content of the story. Thus, Joseph's brothers, upon their release from the Egyptian prison, say to one another that they were being made to suffer because they refused to listen to Joseph when he begged them to release him (Gen 42:41). The text, however, records no such plea from Joseph (Gen 37:23–24). Then there is Reuben reminding his brothers how he counseled at the time that they "do not sin against the lad" (Gen 42:22), yet the text says nothing about an appeal to his brothers not to "sin against the lad" (Gen 37:21–22). In the tradition of good storytelling, the narrator sustains the dramatic tension in Reuben's condemnation of his brothers by inserting details that are not mentioned in the earlier episode. The same is to be said for the so-called discrepancies in Judah's plea to Joseph upon hearing Benjamin is sentenced to serve as a slave in

Egypt. Imploring Joseph to retract the sentence, Judah repeats some of the questions Joseph asked the brothers upon their first meeting. The brothers respond to Joseph's questions by saying that they have a father, "an old man and a child of his old age" (Gen 44:20, JPS), except that in the first meeting with Joseph, no mention is made of an *old* father or a child of *his old age* (Gen 42:11, 13).

These insertions in the Joseph story illustrate the same narrative technique used with Eve and the creature in the garden. God's instructions come to light only when Eve responds to the creature's question, "'Yea, hath God said: Ye shall not eat of any tree of the garden?'" (Gen 3:1, JPS). Eve responds by paraphrasing God's instructions: "'Of the fruit of the trees of the garden we may eat'" (Gen 3:2). But the next verse indicates she is quoting God by prefacing His words with "God said" and showing that all three verbs in the second half of Genesis 3:3 are second-person-plural. When God first warns Adam about the tree (Gen 2:16–17) before the creation of Eve, the second-person-singular of the verb is used; now, however, God uses the plural form in addressing them. It is to be noted that He does not rely upon Adam to repeat His cautionary counsel or to convey the full measure of its gravity; for, no matter how Adam transmits the divine message, his words would not have the same impact. So, God, in speaking to Eve, gives adequate warning about the properties of the tree and its fruit. Why these insertions are made at this point in the story is not clear. Perhaps God wants to warn against adopting any substitute measure for gaining sexual potency, thus forestalling a possible suggestion from the creature that Eve and Adam smear their genitals with the sap of the tree. If such be the case, tapping or pricking the tree would be forbidden.

3.
THE TREE OF PROCREATION

Adam's Foreknowledge

The only knowledge imparted by a tree whose fruit, trunk, and leaves confer fertility would be carnal knowledge. Unlike Mark Twain's Adam, who is told by the woman that she is not an "it," but a "she,"[141] Adam in Hebrew Scripture needs no such instruction. He scrutinizes Eve as keenly as he observes the cattle, the beasts of the field, and the birds of the sky before naming them.[142] His searching examination reveals her distinguishing feature to be sexual.[143] Referring to Eve as *ishah*, "woman," (applying the feminine word-ending to *ish*, "man"), Adam shows how well versed he is in matters anatomical. But his knowledge does not stop with classifying the woman as female. He also knows they were created with different physical characteristics so that, in cleaving together, they appear to be "one flesh."[144] Ultimately, their sexual embrace will result in the woman being called "mother," after bearing her child, and the man being called "father" (Gen 2:24).

No Prohibition, No Transgression

"And the Lord God commanded the man, saying: 'Of every tree of the garden you are free to eat; but as for the tree of knowledge of good and bad, you must not eat of it; for as soon as you eat of it, you shall die'" (Gen 2:16–17, NJPS). This English translation of the Hebrew text does not do justice to the nuanced meanings of Hebrew *tsavah*, "to command," for God does not *prohibit* eating the fruit of the fig tree. In the traditional understanding of the verse, Adam is prohibited from eating the fruit of a certain tree. If he were to do so, he would die on the spot. The English word "commanded" expresses absolute power, but *tsavah* may also mean "to direct," as in the case of the gardener, who directs his assistant to prune trees. Distinct from the imperiousness of "command," the milder "direct," according to Carl Abel, is used when guidance must be given in a situation "too complicated or too new to be mastered by the one directed."[145] Whether the gardener intends to teach or command depends on the gardening knowledge of the assistant. If he knows what his work entails, he will understand "direct" to have the force of "command." But if he knows little or nothing about gardening, either because his assignment is too new or too complicated, he will understand "direct" in the sense of "instruct."

In the Garden of Eden story, Adam fits the role of assistant gardener, who, not having tasted the fruit, is not expected to know everything about the trees he is to tend. So, God, as the instructor, *directs* Adam not to eat the fruit of a particular tree, explaining what will happen to him if he does. God assumes Adam will use his good sense to comprehend the consequence of eating the fruit.

This distinction in the English language is also manifest in the episode where Isaac speaks to Jacob about marrying a Canaanite woman: "So Isaac sent for Jacob and blessed him. He instructed him, saying, 'You shall not take a wife from among the Canaanite women'" (Gen 28:1, NJPS). The translators of NJPS render *tsavah* as "instructed," evidently persuaded that Isaac, blind with age, is too infirm to enforce a command; so, he settles for the *cautionary* role of instructing Jacob not to marry a Canaanite woman. Or, perhaps Jacob, having stolen his father's blessing, demonstrates he is not to be intimidated by a paternal command. Whatever the reason, the translators acknowledge that *tsavah* does not always mean "to command."

Also pertinent to the difference between "command" and "instruct" is what follows. Had nothing followed the instruction "You must not eat of it," the words would have carried the force of a prohibition. Someone issuing a command does not give a reason for an order; but where there is an explanation—"for as soon as you eat of it, you shall die"—God's words are to be understood as instructional. Forewarned, the "assistant gardener" now must decide whether or not to eat the fruit. When Eve and Adam opt to eat the fruit, they are being neither disobedient nor defiant.[146] Rather, they are saying in effect that the procreativity they gain by eating the fruit far outweighs the consequence of death: giving birth to humanity with the birth of their child makes inconsequential their own individual survival.

Dying, Dying ... Dead

God's warning to Adam about the lethality of the fruit has been a stickler for scholars, because they have to reconcile Adam's lifespan of 930 years with a text that is understood to mean that Adam will die on the very day he eats the fruit.[147] And the same with Eve: 130 years after eating the fruit (Gen 4:25, 5:3), she gives birth to Seth and evidently lives for another eight hundred years after bearing other sons and daughters (Gen 5:4). Efforts by scholars to make some sense out of Genesis 2:17 are described by Derek Beattie as "equivocation, flat assertions that black is white, and prodigious feats of intellectual gymnastics ... all, as it seems, on account of a presupposition that God cannot tell a lie."[148] James Barr, while acknowledging God's "slightly shaky moral record" and the "sheer irrationality" of God's threat in Genesis 2:17,[149] perceives the divine command to have been changed from a "threat to kill" to a warning, because God has a change of heart! God now wants Eve and Adam to live, because He knows "there would be no human race" were He to make good on His threat to have Eve and Adam perish instantly.[150] Left unexplained is why God does not think through the ultimate result before "threatening" them with death.

Also unexplained is how death would be imposed. Are Eve and Adam to die from being engulfed in flames by a "fire from Heaven" (Lev. 10:2), or being swallowed up by the earth (Num 26:10, Deut 11:6)?[151] Here Scripture clearly states that God uses fire and the earth as the means of extermination. Significantly, in the Garden of Eden story God is not mentioned as being responsible for the deaths of Eve and Adam; yet scholars who read the two Hebrew words as an emphatic form of "to die" assume that God will cause the couple to die. And why the emphatic form? After all, God does not have to convince Eve and Adam about dying, since they do not question their fate.

The solution offered by those who try to get around the problem of immediate death is no solution at all, for it reads into the Hebrew something which is not there. These exegetes suggest that God is really saying to Adam that as soon as he eats the fruit, he "shall be doomed to die" (Gen 2:17, NJPS). But the threat of being destined to die is meaningless when death is maybe 100 years away in the future, never mind 930 years. Obviously, the intellectual gymnastics of scholars trying to wring sense out of Genesis 2:17 are to no avail, for the unyielding text says nothing about Eve and Adam being *doomed* to die.

For the text to make sense it must be read as a biological statement of fact.

In the phrase *mot tamut*, "dying, you will die," *mot*, the infinitive absolute, is translated as "dying,"[152] foreshadowing what will happen to the sexually potent Eve and Adam, once they begin engaging in sexual intercourse. "Dying" occurs when vital body fluids (shades of Dr. Strangelove) are lost through sexual intercourse. This fluid is also lost in sweating, as when Eve and Adam labor to provide food for themselves and their future family. The *cumulative* effect of these daily "dyings" from coitus and exhausting labor is to deplete the body of its life-sustaining fluid; death then becomes inevitable. Remarkably, Eve and Adam live about nine hundred years before they are finally drained dry of the fluid of life.

What leads to this ebbing of life is reflected in psychological studies on children's ideas of life and death. These studies reveal that children around the age of five develop a vitalist theory of biology, that is to say, they think people are kept alive by a single vital force, much like *chi* in traditional Chinese medicine.[153] The five-year-old may think that a person who does not eat enough gets sick, because his or her vital force is diminished. Death then results when no more of this force is left in the body. Conrad Aiken expresses this idea of daily depletion in *Preludes*: "Give us this day our daily death … ."[154] Eventually, Eve and Adam succumb to the daily draining of their fluid of life.

From Sap/Juice to "Knowledge"

The *da-at,* translated as "knowledge" that is acquired by Eve and Adam upon eating the fruit of the fig tree, has nothing to do with an intellectual understanding of their world. Rather, in its archaic sense,[155] it closely follows the biological development of ideas found in the Greek and Roman concept of knowledge. Thus, *sapientia*, the Latin word for "wisdom, intelligence," is derived from *sapere*, "to be flavored, to have flavor,"[156] which, in turn, is traced to *sapa*, "sap, juice." The sense of taste or flavor is related to fluid, since flavor is stimulated by the fluid in food.[157] Physiologically speaking, Homeric Greeks locate this juice in the blood of the *phrenes*, "lungs," which contain the warm and vaporous *thymos*, "breath,"[158] that deliberates and prompts to action.[159] The *thymos* is not mere breath or air, but something related to blood that interacts with the air one breathes. Locating "juice/blood" in the chest accords with the Greek and Roman belief that locates consciousness and intelligence in the blood of the chest as well as the vapor/breath exhaled from it.[160] Hence, the popular expression—"the breath of intelligence."

Malnutrition diminishes the thymos; adequate nourishment increases it.[161] A prophet divines by what the gods breathe into the thymos, which is vapor from liquid. Prophetic inspiration probably was sought by inhaling vapor or by drinking blood or water, wine or honey. Also involving the senses is the Greek word *aisthanomai*, which developed from "sense-perception, scent, sensation" to "perception, knowledge, understanding."[162] The flavor of food, being in the blood of meat and the juice of fruit,[163] is expressed by the Greek word *chymos*, meaning "juice" of plants and animals as well as "flavor."[164]

The evolution of "sap, juice" to "knowledge, wisdom" in Latin and Greek may be schematized in this fashion: sap, juice–flavor–taste–discrimination–wisdom–knowledge. A similar, abbreviated sequence is found in Hebrew *ta-am*, which progresses from "taste, flavor" to "perception" to "understanding."[165]

These primary meanings of "knowledge" illustrate a parallelism between Hebrew and Greek words linking thought with coitus, as illustrated in the popular phrase "a pregnant thought." Thus:

Hebrew

harah, "to conceive, to be pregnant" [166]

hirheir (from the root *harah*), "to be heated, to entertain impure thoughts"

Greek

apto, "to kindle, set on fire"

"to have intercourse with a woman"

"to grasp with senses, to perceive"[167]

As with the archaic meaning of Hebrew *da-at*, the combination of fluidity and mental activity is present in Greek *menos* and Latin *mens*, "mind."[168] According to the Greeks, *menos* is the thrusting force of a man's sperm that moves with a shooting energy in or from the body.[169] Linking thought and coitus is Latin *mentula*, "penis," which is associated with *mens*, "mind," and Greek *medea*, "thoughts, schemes, genitals."[170]

The Tree of Procreative Fluid

This association between thought, coitus, and sap/juice in the preceding Latin and Greek words, is present in Hebrew *yada*, the verbal form of *da-at*, "knowledge." The element of fluidity inherent in the word "to know" appears in *yada*, "to sweat it out" (Prov 10:9) and "to exude, flow" (Prov 10:32).[171] But it is the archaic meaning of "to discharge fluid in coitus" in Genesis 4 that connects fluid and coitus: "And the man had sexual intercourse with Eve his wife; and she became pregnant and gave birth to Cain ..." (Gen 4:1).

With archaic *yada* meaning "to discharge procreative fluid," the closely related *da-at* is understood as "a discharge of procreative fluid." Consequently, with *da-at* as semen, the name of the celebrated tree in the garden should be "the tree of procreative fluid," or simply "the tree of procreation."[172]

4.

THE TREE OF FRAGRANCE AND LIFE

"Good" as Fragrant

The uniqueness of the fig tree is underscored by its properties of *tov vara*, commonly translated as "good and bad" or "good and evil." These Hebrew words, ranging in definition from "everything"[173] to a description of moral behavior, actually pertain to odor; the Tree of Procreation/Procreative Fluid uniquely sends forth *tov*, a breathtaking, entrancing aroma.

Associating *tov*, "good," with fragrance accords with the Greek pattern of classifying certain smells as "good" (Theophrastus 2:239). "Good" odors, such as the aromata of incense, perfume, spices, and drugs guided the Greeks to what was good to breathe, eat, drink, counter disease, treat wounds, and offer to the gods.[174] Fragrance also emanated from such extraordinary people as the prophet living near the Persian Gulf, who "breathed forth a most pleasant perfume" (Plutarch *Moralia* 5.421B); [175] Alexander, who emits an odor so pleasant that his garments are filled with it (Plutarch *Lives* 7.4.2);[176] and the goddess Demeter with her "fragrant veils," "fragrant bosom," and sweet breath (*Homeric Hymns* 231–80). The Romans spoke of the goddess Flora in like fashion: "A sweet perfume remained; you might know she was a Goddess" (Ovid 5, 375–6); and Virgil noted that Venus's "ambrosial tresses breathed celestial fragrance" (*Aeneid* 402–4). The Egyptians also associated fragrance with their gods. On the reliefs at Der el-Bahri, the wife of Thutmose I is awakened by the fragrance of the god Amon-Re, "which she smelled in the presence of his majesty."[177] But aroma can also reveal a rogue, since each good or bad attribute, according to the Stoics, is itself a substance, "a body gaseous in nature, mingled with that in which it is."[178]

This method of assessing character by smell is reflected in the Latin word *sapio*, "to smell of," as well as "to taste, to have discernment, to be wise."[179] The relationship between "smell" and "taste" is preserved in the term "mouthwatering," which describes the reaction produced by aroma on one's taste buds. The same association between taste, aroma, and perception is also found in 2 Samuel 19:36, where Barzillai uses *tov* and *ra* to explain why he must decline David's invitation to spend his remaining years in Jerusalem. Old age has so dulled his senses, he informs David, that he can no longer tell the difference between the delicacies of the royal table that are *tov*, "delicious, gratifying," and those that are *ra*, "distasteful, displeasing." Nor can he enjoy music and song, so impaired is his hearing. Likewise, in Isaiah 7:15–16, where the subject also is food, *tov* and *ra* are to be understood in the context of 2 Samuel 19:36. Isaiah assures King Ahaz of Judah that the Syro-Ephraimite coalition will be vanquished when Immanuel, weaned at age two or three, has learned to distinguish between foods that are *tov*, "delicious, gratifying," and foods that are *ra*, "distasteful, displeasing." At that age, the child will choose to eat delicacies like curds and honey. For Isaiah, *tov* and *ra* convey no moral implications, for he would hardly expect a child of two or three to have the ethical sensitivity to distinguish between "good" and "evil."[180]

Fragrance in the Story of Esther

Nowhere in Scripture is the association between fragrance and people of extraordinary qualities more pronounced than in the story of Esther. Were it not for the importance attached to fragrance, Esther might not have been selected as queen, and the fate of her people might have ended tragically. The story records in detail the year's preparatory beauty treatment prescribed for all contestants vying to replace the deposed Queen Vashti. So consequential a role does fragrance play in the selection process that something more than the mere creation of a pleasant aroma is to be ascribed to aromatic oils and spices.

The significance of fragrance is underscored in the advice given to King Ahasuerus by his attendants on how to proceed with the selection of a successor to Queen Vashti: "Let there be sought for the king young virgins fair to look on; and let the king appoint officers in all the provinces of his kingdom, that they may gather together all the fair young virgins unto Shushan the castle, to the house of the women, unto the custody of Hegai the king's chamberlain, keeper of the women; and let their ointments be given them; and let the maiden that pleaseth the king be queen instead of Vashti" (Esth 2:2–4, JPS).

The mention of perfumed ointments—note that nothing is said about apparel, jewelry, or coiffure—establishes fragrance as the single most important factor in the selection process. From the time the young women are assembled in the custody of Hegai to the time they present themselves to the king, they are to be immersed in perfumed oils and ointments for over a year: six months with oil of myrrh and six months with perfumes and other ointments (Esth 2:12). Equally significant is Hegai's treatment of Esther. He is so taken with her that he appoints seven maidens to wait upon her, furnishes her with "her cosmetics and her rations" (Esth 2:9), and advances her to the choicest apartment in the house of women. Emphasis on the fragrance of perfumed ointment is so marked in these few verses that one must ask if fragrance is the sole standard for judging who is "better" than the former queen (Esth 1:19, JPS).

Selecting a Queen

Before this question can be answered, one must determine what being "better" is not. First, being "better" does not mean better looking. If the narrator intended beauty to be the sole determinant, he would have used the same phrase he used previously to express beauty, namely, *tovat mareh* (Esth 2:2). The omission of this phrase suggests a standard other than beauty. Second, being "better" does not mean that a contestant's disposition is better than that of ill-tempered Vashti, since it is a given that each young woman will be obliging, courteous, and gracious to enhance her chance at the throne. Ahasuerus would have to be the most discriminating of kings to detect among these ingratiating beauties the subtle gradations of character that determine who is the "sweetest."

Nor does "better" refer to bedtime frolicking. No matter that the power of Ahasuerus extends over 127 provinces, stretching from India to Ethiopia, or that his wealth is measured by sumptuous banquets, golden table service, and couches of silver and gold, that potent a potentate he is not. Neither his sexual capacity nor his erotic desire is so overpowering, judging by the thirty days he absented himself from Queen Esther's bedside, that he can perform the role of sexual partner night ... after night ... after night ... and still be responsive enough to select as queen the one virgin who best excites a sorely tried libido.[181] But then the text does not say that the king has to engage in sexual intercourse with every contestant. All it says is that each maiden goes into the king's private quarters in the evening and leaves in the morning for the second house of women, supervised by the king's chamberlains in charge of concubines. Whatever the criteria, the king's bed is not the testing grounds for determining the winner.

Since "better" is not being more attractive, more congenial, or more erotically stimulating, the word *tovah*, heretofore translated as "better," must refer to the one factor repeatedly stressed in the narrative—*fragrance*. The king is advised that the crown be given to the maiden whose potential for royalty is to be perceived in her aroma. With such a touchstone, the king's one worry is catching a head cold with the concomitant stuffy nose.

The selection process evidently allows for a "call back" (Esth 2:14) of those particularly seductive young women from the House of Concubines to grace the king's bed. This sidenote supports the interpretation that aroma is the sole criterion for judging these maidens. Were the king to choose as his queen the most erotically stimulating, why the need for sexual diversion with an "also ran"? But with fragrance as the criterion, the king is not averse to sampling the sexual favors of those contestants who, while not as "regally" aromatic as Esther, are apparently more sexually provocative.

Of course, the king may have fallen in love with Esther at first sight; for the text clearly states that "the king loved Esther more than all the other women" (Esth 2:17, NJPS). Were this a case of true love, it still would not explain what being "better" is, unless Esther is "better" at causing a mighty surge of affection to well up in the king's heart—a highly unlikely possibility. To believe that Ahasuerus succumbs that easily and quickly to the charms of a woman is to stretch the limits of credulity. A ruler who regards his former wife as a prized possession, to be displayed in somewhat the same fashion as his costly drapes and gold inlay, and who keeps in the wings for future use the more sexually alluring maidens is not a person who falls in love at first sight, or even at fifteenth sight. Though the Hebrew text reads that the king "loved" Esther more than anyone else, it appears that the word *ahav*, "to love," conveys in this instance something other than what today is meant by "love."

"Love" as Fragrance

That *ahav*, "to love," can mean something else is evident from the warning the fatherly figure in Proverbs gives the young man: stay clear of the lascivious temptress, and seek sexual pleasure only from one's wife—"Let her breasts satisfy you at all times; be infatuated with love of her always" (Prov 5:19, JPS).

The advice could not be any more specific: the young husband will find his wife's breasts so sexually stimulating that he'll not seek the company of the seductress. But in the next line the explicitness of breasts seemingly is abandoned for the abstraction of love. One would expect otherwise, that the speaker would continue in the same vein by offering yet another aspect of heightened sexual pleasure with one's wife. Actually, the speaker does precisely that, once *ahavah* is understood as "fragrance" and *shagah* as "to be wrapped up in" or "addicted to."[182] The fatherly figure tells the young husband that he will become addicted to the particular scent emitted by his wife in the act of lovemaking.

This heady, intoxicating aroma can come from perfumes employed specifically to rouse men to a high state of sexual excitement, as with the Greeks, who employed scented unguents and salves for erotic stimulation."[183] Or, this addicting fragrance can come from a lubricant secreted by the young man's wife. The young lover in Song of Songs refers to this lubricant when he declares to the maiden that the aroma of her 'oils' exceeds that of any spice (Cant 4:10); and his beloved speaks of *her* scent ('my nard') as pervasive in the presence of her lover.[184] This fragrant concomitant of lovemaking also is mentioned in ancient Egyptian love poetry: "The heavens pant with storms. / He does not remove it. / That she may bring you her fragrance, / an odor which overflows to cause those who are present to become intoxicated."[185]

These examples from Greek, Egyptian, and Hebrew literature suggest that *ahavah*, "love," in Prov 5:19 is to be translated as "fragrance." When understood in this way, the verb *ahav* in Isaac's request that Esau hunt wild game means something other than "like" or "love": "... and make me savory food, such as I love, and bring it to me" (Gen 27:4, JPS). Love today can emphasize fondness for a certain food. Thus, one "loves" pizza or ice cream. In Hebrew Scripture, however, "loving" to eat something means more than fondness for a special food. What Isaac "loves" about this food is its taste and smell, which are linked together in the Hebrew word *rei-ach*, "flavor, scent, odor."[186] The word "love" expresses the same sense experience of aroma/taste as used in the Esther story. Here the narrator alludes to the experience of inhaling a pleasant aroma by his use of *ahav*, "to love." With *tov*, "good" or "better" as it relates to fragrance, it is Esther's scent that the king "loved ... above all women."

The importance of aromata in the Esther story is underscored by the names of the principal protagonist—Hadassah/Esther (Esth 2:7). Hadassah is the feminine of *hadas*, "myrtle," and the Medic meaning for "myrtle," traced through the Old Persian, is *astra*, as found in the name Esther.[187] Thus, in the phrase "Hadassah, that is, Esther," Esther appropriately is given the name "myrtle," since the gum and gum resin from myrtle were used in the ancient Near East to manufacture perfume and incense.[188]

Tov is translated as "fragrant" in *hashemen hatov*, "fragrant oil" (Isa 39:2, NJPS), and *kaneh hatov* as "fragrant cane" (Jer 6:20, NJPS). In Song of Songs the rendition of "spiced wine" (Cant 7:10, NEB) is to be preferred over "the best wine," because wines in the ancient east Mediterranean world were blended with spices. An analysis of Greek wine found in sealed glass flasks deposited in tombs shows that people blended their wine with sweet-scented substances to obtain a pleasant-smelling beverage with the consistency of syrup.[189] Rabbinic Hebrew also knows of perfumed or spiced wine.[190]

Finally, understanding *tov* as "fragrant" in the refrain of the creation story of Genesis 1 buttresses my theory that the waters of the Flood were meant to cleanse an initially sweet-smelling world of its malodorous pollution.[191]

The Fragrant Fig Tree

That *tov*, "good," pertains to the fragrance of the fig tree is found in the fable of Jotham's fig tree, which refuses the honor of kingship over all the trees on the grounds of not wanting to leave *matki*, "my sweetness," and *tnuvati hatovah*, "my good/sweet fruit."[192] Associating sweet scent with the fig tree continues to this day with the *ficus sycomorus* of Jericho, a fig tree with a strong fragrance and intensely sweet fruit.[193] The fragrance of the fig tree becomes particularly pronounced when the opening of its buds sends out an odor much like sweetly perfumed incense.[194]

"Seeing" and "Glowing"

Also substantiating *tov* as "fragrant" are the other fruit trees in the garden: "And from the ground the Lord God caused to grow every tree that was pleasant to the sight and good for food ..." (Gen 2:9, NJPS). What seems at first glance to be highly unusual is the order of the properties of the trees: appearance comes first ("pleasant to the sight"), then edibility ("good for food"). One would think the narrator would mention edibility before appearance, for food is fundamental to life. That he does not seems to say that he places more importance on appearance than edibility, unless *nechmad lemareh,* "pleasant to the sight," relates directly to edibility—which it does.

First, *mareh*, from *ra-ah*, "to see," can mean something other than "sight," once it is acknowledged that the relationship between "gazing" and "glowing," present in other Hebrew words for "to see, look," is at work here as well. Thus:

> *navat*, "to see, look," with an original meaning of "to shine, be bright" [195]
>
> *tsuts*, "to shine, sparkle," with its intensive (hiphil) of "to gaze, peer" [196]

This sense of *mareh* as "shining, glowing" is used to describe the cloud of "glory" enveloping Sinai: "And the appearance of the glory of the Lord was like a devouring fire on the top of the mount in the eyes of the children of Israel" (Exod 24:17, JPS). Since the "glory" of God is mentioned in the preceding verse, *mareh* as "appearance" adds nothing to the meaning of the sentence. Furthermore, the devouring fire is not likened to the "appearance" but to the "glory," for it is the brilliance, the gleaming quality of the "glory" that looks like a devouring fire. In this instance, *mareh* makes far more sense as "brilliance" or "glow": "And the brilliance of the glory of the Lord was like a devouring fire."

This cloud of glory, dazzling the eye with its fierce brightness, is reflected in the glow on Moses's face when he appears again before the Israelites with the terms of the covenant. Moses is infused with this glow when he is addressed by God, who presumably gazes upon him while hidden in the cloud enveloping the peak.[197] God's luminous presence also manifests itself in the phenomenon of a bush that seemingly burns but is not consumed. Moses describes this spectacle with the word *mareh*, traditionally rendered as "sight": "'I will turn aside now and see this great sight, why the bush is not burnt'" (Exod 3:3, JPS). But "sight" fails to convey the concrete descriptiveness so favored by the narrator. Only when *mareh* is rendered as "brilliance" or "glow" is specificity restored. Moses turns aside to gaze in wonderment upon the brilliant bush that is not consumed by the fire.[198]

Eden's Trees of Brightness

With *mareh* rendered as "brilliance" in the Garden of Eden story, the Tree of Procreation radiates a dazzling brightness that recalls the ancient Near Eastern myth of the garden of the gods, where magical trees sparkle with jeweled fruit.[199] The *Epic of Gilgamesh* speaks of shining trees bearing carnelian and lapis lazuli growing in the garden of the goddess Siduri;[200] and in the Mesopotamian nether world of Eridu, the trunk of the Tree of Life is studded with metal and precious stones, glistening with "the sheen of its magic power."[201]

The same folkloristic tradition that depicts trees gleaming with carnelian, topaz, emerald, and sapphire is preserved in Ezekiel's "garden of God" (Ezek 28:13). Evidently the narrator in the Garden of Eden story conforms to the outline of the ancient Near Eastern myth that associates shining, bejeweled trees with the garden of the gods, except for one modification: Eden's gleaming trees yield fruit that is *tov*, "good" for eating. Unlike the cherubim in Ezekiel's garden or the Greek gods and goddesses in *The Iliad*, who "eat not bread neither drink flaming wine, wherefore they are bloodless and are called immortals" (5.340), the humanity of the first couple is underscored by trees that provide the nourishment of life.

Fragrance and Edibility

The dual meaning of *tov* as "fragrant" and "edible" also appears in Genesis 3:6, where the creature tries to get Eve to eat the fruit of the Tree of Procreation. The creature begins by asserting that God instructed Eve and Adam not to eat of any tree in the garden. Not so, says Eve. They are permitted to eat of every tree except the tree in the midst of the garden; for they will die if they eat its fruit. The tempter then tries another line of argument: God knows that on the day they eat of it, their eyes will brighten with the life-engendering sap of fertility. This riposte moves Eve to compare the fruit of this tree with the fruit of the other trees; for only then does she perceive that "the tree was good for food" (Gen 3:6, JPS).

But how does Eve know the tree is "good" for food? Surely not by touching and squeezing, for what can be learned of a fruit's edibility by touching? Perhaps then by looking? Not really. Comparing the fig's size, color, and outward texture with that of apples, pomegranates, or dates says nothing about edibility. So, by process of elimination, Eve determines its edibility by smell, as illustrated by Arthur Miller's Eve in *The Creation of the World*:

> LUCIFER, *offering her his apple.* Take a bite, Eve, and everything will clear up.
>
> EVE, *accepts the apple, looks at it.* It smells all right.
>
> LUCIFER. Of course. It *is* all right.[202]

In the Genesis story, Eve puts the fig to the smell test by comparing its aroma with the fragrance emanating from the other fruit trees. Unable to detect any marked difference between the aroma of the fruit of the Tree of Procreation and the other trees, she concludes "that the tree was good for food" (Gen 3:6); in other words, the fruit is safe to eat.

Just as *ra-ah*, "to see," connotes "to perceive" in Genesis 3:6, so does it also have the same connotation in the episode where Jacob/Israel is visited on his deathbed by Joseph and his two sons. The text reads: "And Israel beheld Joseph's sons … " (Gen 48:8, JPS). Yet, the following verse reads: "the eyes of Israel were dim from age, so that he could not see" (Gen 48:10, JPS). Since cognition depends on something other than Jacob's sense of sight, *ra-ah* must mean "to perceive."

This connection between perception and the act of smelling is evident to this day in such expressions as "to nose about," "to sniff around," and in the French *sentir*, "to smell, perceive, feel."[203] In his essay "On Smell," Lewis Thomas explains that "the act of smelling something, anything, is remarkably like the act of thinking itself … . The cells that do the smelling are themselves proper brain cells, the only neurons whose axons carry information picked up at first hand in the outside world."[204] In *Cat On A Hot Tin Roof*, Tennessee Williams illustrates the workings of these neurons in less scientific terms when Big Daddy, confronting the members of the family plotting behind his back, alerts his son Brick to the obnoxious *odor of mendacity* in the room.[205] For George Orwell smell serves as an index of integrity. Comparing Gandhi, the politician, with the other leading politicians of his time, he notes "how clean a smell he has managed to leave behind."[206]

Conclusion: the fragrance of the Tree of Procreation convinces Eve that its fruit is edible.

The Moisture of the Fruit

Pushed by the creature into assessing the edibility of the fruit of the Tree of Procreation, Eve finds the fruit to be "a delight to the eyes" (Gen 3:6, NJPS). Since Eve already has concluded that the fig is edible, why does the narrator add that the fruit is also a delight to the eyes? So what if Eve is taken with the shape and color of the fig; why take special note of its appeal, since, seemingly, this aesthetic observation adds nothing to the story?

Obviously, what Eve sees in the fruit has nothing to do with beauty or seductiveness. [207, 208] Rather, the narrator is commenting on the ocular effect it has upon a person eating a fig. When Eve speaks of the *ta-avah* of the eyes, she does not do so because hunger drives her to think of eating the fruit. If such were the case, she would have plucked the fruit of any of the other trees in the garden. No, her reason for eating the fig is to acquire the glistening fluid she sees reflected in the eyes of the creature. *Ta-avah*, as used in this context, refers specifically to the "fluid, moisture" reflected in glistening eyes.

My reading of *ta-avah* as "fluid, moisture" of the eyes is reflected in the story of the riffraff who accompany the Israelites through the desert. At some point during their trek, they "felt a gluttonous craving …" presumably for meat (Num 11:4, NJPS). They make known their craving by loud lamentation, as borne out in the second part of the verse: "… and the children of Israel also wept on their part" (Num 11:4, JPS). The use of "also" indicates that the Israelites vent their feelings in much the same way as the rabble—they wail. Pouring out the moisture of their eyes in the form of tears best expresses the intensity of their craving.

So too does *ta-avah* as "moisture, sap" in Psalm 106 describe the dehydration suffered by the Israelites in their trek through the Sinaitic desert: "And they lost their moisture in the desert …" (Psa 106:14). In desperation, they petition (*lenasot*) God to cast out the "wasting" (dehydration) from their soul (Psa 106:15). *Razon* as "dryness" in Isaiah 10:16 is contrasted with *shemen*, "oil," which is "seed," "the liquid of life and strength," when anointing the head.[209] The anointed head receives the life and strength inherent in the "seed," which is then absorbed by the nefesh, "the soul/thymos," the vaporous breath which is diminished by an ill-nourished body.[210] So, *razon* as "dryness" describes a soul dangerously depleted of moisture.

God replenishes the *ta-avah*, "the moisture/sap of life," to prevent the soul's sap of life from drying up by unleashing winds that force battered migratory birds to drop exhausted into the camp of the Israelites. This fresh meat replenishes the *ta-avah*, the sap or fluid of life of the Israelites (Psa 78:29), thereby ridding them of their bad breath.[211] No longer will the Israelites emit the stench of the dying.

These examples of *ta-avah* as "fluid, moisture," support the premise that Eve regards the clear liquid exuding from the "eye" of the fig at the time of maturity as kindred to the seed/sap in a person's body. Such varieties as Dottato, Lob Injir, Rixford, and Castle Kennedy all show this drip of pellucid gum.[212] "When Castle Kennedy is 'within a few days of being ripe,'" observes one authority, "'a clear honey-looking substance of exquisite flavor commences to drop from the eye of each fruit. When quite ripe this substance becomes somewhat viscid, hanging like an elongated dewdrop, from half an inch to three-quarters in length, clear as crystal, giving a very remarkable appearance to the fruit.'"[213] It may be inferred from the narrator's use of *ta-avah* that the figs on the Tree of Procreative Fluid also exude globules of syrup, thus making its fruit mouth-wateringly attractive. This drop of clear sap must have seemed like a tear drop, as with the Spanish, who described the perfect fig as "'a neck for the hangman, a robe for the beggar, a tear for the penitent.'"[214]

But this is not all that Eve observes. There are the cracks in the skin of the fig that allow "the juices to exude and to stand out like drops of dew."[215] Indeed, the *Book of Baruch* (IV) in the Apocrypha, (late second- or early first-century BCE) focuses on these cracks in the skin of the fig in the story of Jeremiah, who is being led away captive at the fall of Jerusalem. He prevails upon God to permit Abimelech to leave the city on condition that he provides himself with a basket of figs for the sick. Abimelech picks these figs in the garden of Agrippa and then falls asleep under a tree with his head on the basket. Sixty-six years later he awakens, unaware of the lapse of time, to find the figs in the same condition as when he picked them, with juice dripping from the cracks in the skin.[216]

Eve gazes upon the shape and color of the ripe fig. The teardrops of clear syrup and juice oozing out of the checked skin of ripe figs convince her that this glowing, fragrant Tree of Procreation provides the very stuff of life. All that is required now is that it be eaten!

5.
THE TREE OF STENCH AND DEATH

Evil and Stench

The sweet aroma of the Tree of Procreation poses a troublesome question for Eve. How can a tree of such fragrance be called *ra*, whose primary meaning is to give off a fecal odor?[217] In Hebrew Scripture, *ra*, "bad," is associated with stench, as in *zanach*, "to smell bad,"[218] used by Hosea to express the enormity of Israel's sinfulness. There is also *shachat*, "to act corruptly, lawlessly," whose origin is to be traced to *yeshach*, "fecal matter."[219] This association between stench and evil is also found in the Greek language. Greek *kakos*, "bad, evil," is related to *kakke*, "fecal matter,"[220] and Theophrastus links putridity with evil when he observes that "anything which is decomposing has an evil odor …" (*Concerning Odours* 3.2:329). In contemporary times, immorality has been expressed by "stink" and by the German *Dreck*, "excrement."[221] The pervasiveness of the foul smell of evil reaches the very heavens, Othello tells Desdemona in answer to her question about what sin she committed: "'What committed! Heaven stops the nose at it'" (*Othello*, 4.2.170). For the rector of Stephen Dedalus's Jesuit day school, the foul smell of evil permeates hell, where "all the filth of the world, all the offal and scum of the world" fill it with an intolerable odor.[222] Over the millennia and despite cultural differences, the foulness of fecal matter has been, and continues to be, associated with foul play.

Death and Stench

The association of stench with death, so unmistakable when the corpse gives off a deadly odor,[223] or when noxious vapors emanate from the unburied victims of a plague,[224] compounds this arboreal paradox. Illustrative of the horrid smells that can be fatal to those who inhale them are the trees that kill people "by the vile stench" of their flowers (Lucretius, *De rerum Natura* 6.787), and the miasma of certain villages in early modern Europe of the 1600s.[225] Moreover, a disagreeable odor determines the gravity of a wound or disease, as with Job, who, acknowledging the severity of his condition, says that he has become like the stench of dung to his wife and his neighbors (Job 19:17).

Stench, the aftereffect of physical ailments that culminate in death, attests to humanity's dependence upon a sense of smell for survival. Down through the ages people have lived by the maxim that to safeguard life one must avoid the "bad" smells of decay and putridity. Margie Profet, while associated with the Division of Biochemistry and Molecular Biology of the University of California (Berkeley), theorized that the olfactory sense of a woman in the early stages of pregnancy becomes highly acute to smells given off, for example, by the toxins with which vegetables fight off herbivores. The pregnant woman's nausea, often followed by vomiting, quite likely is indicative of her ability to sense food that might be dangerous to the embryo.[226] Thus, from humanity's earliest beginnings, the sensory message has been unequivocal: avoid the malodorous upon pain of death. Only the "good" odor, heightened by the knowledge of aromata in the medicinal arts of the ancient Mediterranean world, promotes healing and enhances life.

Beneficial Properties of Fragrance

Aromatic gum resins were used extensively both to heal and to counter the unbearable odor of festering wounds.[227] Their nondecaying properties made these gum resins particularly important as antiseptics for preventing wounded flesh from decomposing. What the ancients learned by trial and error some five thousand years ago has been confirmed by laboratory experiment: myrrh, an aromatic gum resin, acts as a bacteriostatic against *Staphylococcus aureus*, a typical wound bacterium, and other gram-positive bacteria.[228]

Aromatic fumes also were used by the ancients for medicinal purposes. The burning of gums, spices, and other aromatic substances served as decontaminants by inhibiting the growth and spread of microorganisms. In an age that knew nothing of microorganisms, the ancients burned incense and cedar wood to rid themselves of mice, moths, and other pests.[229]

In the house of the deceased, incense was burned to rid the dwelling of its noxious character.[230] From painful experience, people realized that the air they breathed, whether in the house of one who died of a disease or an entire village felled by a plague, could be "corrupted." To prevent succumbing to the same illness, people followed a procedure similar to that used by Noah. After all the living creatures leave the ark, Noah burns a combination of woods that gives off a pleasing odor (Gen 8:20–21), much like the "sweet savor" Utnapishtim, the Babylonian flood survivor, produces from a combination of cane, cedar wood, and myrtle.[231] Aromatic wood is burned in areas devastated by the mass extermination of life to fumigate the land of any lingering, pestilential traces of the stench of death. A similar rationale accounts for the means used to destroy Sodom and Gommorah: God burns sulfur instead of aromatic fumes to disinfect the area of the physical pollution that befouled these towns.[232] Likewise, in Homer's *The Odyssey*, Odysseus asks for fire and brimstone to fumigate the house after killing the suitors (22.481–2).

Laboratory experiments have confirmed the beneficial effect of burning gum olibanum, gum glabanum, storax myrrh, saffron, and cinnamon, the fumes of which prevented the growth of freshly transplanted bacteria.[233] The record is clear: fragrance, whether applied directly to a suppurating wound or released through fumigation, signified health and life-enhancement for the inhabitants of the ancient Mediterranean world. Stench prognosticated illness and death.

The Olfactory Sense of the Soul

Moses, in addressing the Israelites, recognizes the capacity of a person to distinguish between life-enhancing and life-diminishing conditions through one's sense of smell: "'See, I have set before thee this day life and good, death and evil … therefore choose life'" (Deut 30:15, 19, JPS). With *tov* understood as "fragrance" and *ra* as "evil/bad/stench, the conduct of the Israelites will determine whether they are to enjoy the fragrance of life or suffer the foul odor of death. As with the Greek philosopher Heraclitus, the soul determines what is good or bad for the body by distinguishing between these antithetical smells.[234] It may be assumed from the close resemblance between the Greek *thymus*, "soul," and the Hebrew *nefesh*, "soul,"[235] that the *nefesh*, "soul," is endowed with the capacity to distinguish between the perfumed and the putrid. Adam, created as a *nefesh chaiyah*, "a living soul" (Gen 2:17), has the capacity to make such an olfactory distinction. That Eve also has been endowed with a soul is clear from the narrator's use of the one phrase male supremacists paradoxically invoke to relegate woman to inferior status: *eizer kenegdo*, traditionally translated as "a fitting helper for him" (Gen 2:18, NJPS).

A Fitting Helper

God's observation that "'it is not good that man should be alone'" (Gen 2:18, JPS) has been interpreted as meaning that man, created for sociability,[236] will be provided with a suitable companion in his solitude,[237] or that God creates woman only after Adam fails to find a mate among the animals.[238] But Adam's problem is more than loneliness. As the only human being out there, he has nobody to mate. So, God responds to Adam's plight by making an *eizer* for him.

The biblical translations generally define *eizer* as "helper," but what is there to help with in a garden that does not call for heavy lifting? No, what Adam needs is a mate, not a helper. The narrator acknowledges as much with the word *eizer*. As used in Genesis 2:18, *eizer* is derived from the same root as *azarah*, "enclosure,"[239] and both are synonymous with "form, frame."[240] The same etymological development may be seen in the Latin word *forma*. From a root meaning "to bring together, hold," *forma* proceeds from its primary meaning of "holder, container," to "frame, case, enclosure," to "mold, model, last," and, finally, to "form, shape."[241] Current usage reflects how "frame," an enclosing border, denotes "form, structure."[242] With "frame" referring to the build or makeup of a person's body, *eizer*, as "frame, form," speaks of the *form* of Eve's body: God creates a woman with a body frame similar to that of man.[243]

Implicit in my definition of *eizer* is the idea of correspondence. The female frame formed by God will correspond with Adam's frame in every respect. Therefore, translating *k'negdo* as "corresponding to him" in the phrase *eizer k'negdo* (Gen 2:18) is redundant. Rather, emphasis should be placed upon the root form of *k'negdo*, namely *neged*, whose original meaning is "in front."[244] J. L. Palache notes that the literal meaning of *k'negdo*, "according to his *neged*," is probably still preserved in Genesis 2:18 and 2:20 and "refers to the physiological difference between man and animal with regard to cohabitation."[245] By focusing on the "in front" part of the body,[246] namely, the genital area,[247] the narrator is saying that God's *eizer k'negdo* will be a female figure, whose frontal genital area is perfectly suited for coitus with the male figure. This phrase, *eizer k'negdo*, repeated in Genesis 2:20, follows Adam's act of giving names to the livestock, the game fowl, and the game animals. But here the narrator stresses the "in front" part of Adam's body to clarify Adam's relationship with the animals he names. The narrator expands upon the nature of this relationship by rejecting the idea that God blunders in creating Adam's mate or that Adam searches for his mate among the livestock and game animals.

As for God "succeeding" in creating a matching female figure only after a second try, no explanation is needed, because no explanation is called for. When God declares His intention to provide Adam with an identical female figure as his mate, He first provides sustenance for Adam's projected family by creating game animals and fowl to supplement the previously created livestock. That done, the livestock and the newly created game are endowed with the capacity to reproduce when Adam names them with the formulaic *kara sheim*, "to give a name," (chapter 13).

Significantly, the narrator then adds *ul'adam lo-matsa eizer k'negdo*, usually translated as "but for Adam no fitting helper was found" (Gen 2:20, NJPS). This translation has been taken to infer that Adam searches among the newly created game animals for his mate. But since he knows nothing of God's intention to create a mate for him, why make such an inference? Adam's assignment is to give names to the livestock and the newly created game. The narrator adds that Adam does not find a matching mate among the animals; in other words, the narrator is saying "for the record" that Adam has not gone through the motions of copulating with any of these animals. Motivating the narrator to make such a statement is the role played by the hybrid *nachash*, the third party in the garden. The narrator uses the phrase *eizer k'negdo* in Genesis 2:20b to state unequivocally that Adam, though not yet endowed with procreative fluid, is not responsible in any way for siring this creature.

But Adam's scrutiny of the creatures parading before him makes him conscious of his need for the companionship of another human being.[248] It is only when God produces woman as his counterpart that Adam exclaims: "This—this female—at last is a creation corresponding to me."[249]

Accepting woman as his life's companion, Adam will cleave to her as one flesh (Gen 2:24), so closely are they to be entwined physically. Centuries later, Galen, the Greek physician who wrote extensively on the human body, describes the female and male sex organs as perfectly matched for such entwining: "All the parts, then, that men have, women have too, the difference between them lying in only one thing ... that in women the parts are within (the body), whereas in men they are outside in the region of the perineum. Consider first whichever ones you please, turn inward, so to speak, and fold double the man's, and you will find them the same in both in every respect" (*On the Usefulness of the Parts of the Body* 2:268). After commenting on how each organ can be changed into the corresponding organ of the opposite sex, Galen concludes: "In fact, you could not find a single male part left over that had not simply changed its position; for the parts that are inside in woman are outside in man."[250]

Such correspondence of parts allows the narrator to assert that the woman is Adam's physical counterpart[251]—a correspondence that presupposes Eve's possession of a *nefesh*, "soul," for distinguishing between the perfumed and the putrid. Consequently, Eve can be expected to exercise the same degree of caution in avoiding the stench of death that Moses expects of all Israelites when he urges them to choose life and good.

Sniffing before Eating

Eve, though puzzled perhaps, by a fig tree that is supposed to give off both a perfumed aroma and a stench, is not reduced to passivity. Unable to detect any odor of decay in the fruit of the Tree of Procreation, she makes her move. In her world of fragrance and stench, the absence of any foul-smelling substance signifies life, not death. So, the creature's assurance that she will not die confirms what she already has determined by herself: the fruit of the fragrant tree is life-enhancing.

To appreciate the dialogue between Eve and the creature, careful note must be taken of the narrator's sequence of words and events. Eve does not respond immediately to the assurance of the creature. Presumably, she first sniffs the fruit to ascertain its aroma (Gen 3:6). Only after she is convinced by its fragrance that the antithetical characteristics of life and death are not present in the same object does she eat the fig.

Similarities between Eve and Pandora

Certain subtleties in the story of Eve come to light when contrasted with Hesiod's story of a paradisiac community, where never-aging men live apart "from cruel diseases that bring death to men."[252] The placidity of this existence changes when Zeus, head of the Greek pantheon, orders a woman—Pandora—to be made expressly for these mortals. Hephaistos, engaged by Zeus to manufacture her body parts and physical attributes, mixes earth with water to create this goddess-like creature. Then Athena teaches her arts; Aphrodite gives her loving and alluring attributes; and Hermes provides her with a treacherous mind. Endowing Pandora with these physical and mental attributes, according to Pucci, results in a being "beautiful in its outward aspect but pernicious inside."[253] Epimetheus, ignoring Prometheus's warning never to accept any of Zeus's gifts for man, delivers to this paradisiac community the treacherous Pandora, who then removes the lid of the great vase containing all the ills that will bring humanity to the grave.[254]

The similarity of the stories of Eve and Pandora is striking.[255] First, both women are formed after the creation of man, and both are said to be responsible for introducing death into a paradisiac setting, though Eve is not described as created with a treacherous mind. Second, the rivalry between Prometheus and Zeus is matched to some extent by a devious creature, who controverts God's warning that eating the fruit of the Tree of Procreation will result in death. Scripture does not say the creature considers God a rival, but its impertinence in impugning God's words smacks of rivalry. Third, just as man comes to understand the real nature of Pandora only after he accepts her,[256] so too do Eve and Adam fully appreciate the effects of the fig only after they eat it.

Dissimilarities between Eve and Pandora

The two stories differ, however, with respect to God's conduct and the introduction of death. God, far from trying to persuade Eve to eat of the fruit of the Tree of Procreation, does just the opposite: He forewarns Eve and Adam of the dire consequences of eating the fruit. Zeus, on the other hand, does not tell Epimetheus why he wants Pandora constructed, for were he to do so, he would be disclosing his scheme to afflict humanity with senescence, disease, and death.

The introduction of death is the second fundamental difference between these two stories. In the Hesiod story, death operates as an outside force after Pandora releases the lethal ills from the vase; in Hebrew Scripture, death is the "inside" force working from within. Once Eve and Adam eat the fruit of the Tree of Procreation, they trigger the process that eventually will lead to their deaths. Also, by linking death with procreation, the Eden story parallels the literature of the ancient Mediterranean world by associating stench and death with the onset of menstruation and seminal production.

6.
SEXUALITY AND TOXICITY

Death and Menstruation

Menstruation in Pliny's *Natural History*, the scientific sourcebook of the Middle Ages, is a force to be feared. The assiduous Roman cataloger of natural phenomena observes that nothing is "more remarkable than the monthly flux of women" (2:549). For good reason does Pliny use the word "remarkable" with regard to menstrual blood: "Contact with it turns new wine sour, crops touched by it become barren, grafts die, seeds in gardens are dried up, the fruit of trees fall off, the bright surface of mirrors in which it is merely reflected is dimmed, the edge of steel and the gleam of ivory are dulled, hives of bees die, even bronze and iron are at once seized by rust, and a horrible smell fills the air; to taste it drives dogs mad and infects their bites with an incurable poison."[257]

Women with such awesome power can take on the elements—and do. "First of all, they say that hailstorms and whirlwinds are driven away if menstrual fluid is exposed to the very flashes of lightning; that stormy weather too is thus kept away, and that at sea exposure, even without menstruation, prevents storms ... if this female power should issue when the moon or sun is in eclipse, it will cause irremediable harm; no less harm if there is no moon; at such seasons sexual intercourse brings disease and death upon the man; purple too is tarnished then by the woman's touch" (2:55–7). As to be expected, extreme caution is advised, otherwise the anticipated blessing can become a curse: "Care must be taken that they do not do so at sunrise, for the crop dries up, they say, the young vines are irremediably harmed by the touch, and rue and ivy, plants of the highest medicinal power, die at once" (2:55–7).

The menstruous woman is not always destructive; she can also be a force for good: "But at any other time of menstruation, if women go round the cornfield naked, caterpillars, worms, beetles and other vermin fall to the ground" (2:55–7). Aside from the benefits accruing to agriculture, the menstruous woman performs wondrous cures for the sick: "... by her touch a woman in this state relieves scrofula, parotid tumors, superficial abscesses, erysipelas, boils and eye-fluxes" (2:59).

It is to be inferred from the Levitical quarantine imposed upon a woman during her menstrual period that Pliny reflects beliefs then current in the east Mediterranean world:

> When a woman has a discharge, her discharge being blood from her body, she shall remain in her impurity seven days; whoever touches her shall be unclean until evening. Anything that she lies on during her impurity shall be unclean; and anything that she sits on shall be unclean. Anyone who touches her bedding shall wash his clothes, bathe in water, and remain unclean until evening; and anyone who touches any object on which she has sat shall wash his clothes, bathe in water, and remain unclean until evening. Be it the bedding or be it the object on which she has sat, on touching it he shall be unclean until evening. And if a man lies with her, her impurity is communicated to him; he shall be unclean seven days, and any bedding on which he lies shall become unclean. (Lev 15:19–24, NJPS)

These beliefs are not to be explained away as the concoctions of benighted ancients, since beliefs current in some parts of the modern world also associate the menstruous woman with the unnatural. For example, fresh flowers touched by a menstruous woman wither; bread dough kneaded by her does not rise; and in the great French perfumery manufacturing centers, she is not allowed to work during her menstrual period.[258]

How is it that such stories continue to circulate? Is it because superstitions regarding women never die? Or, is it because the threatened male, desperate to preserve some semblance of masculine pride, circulates these stories as a sop to his bruised machismo? While superstition and masculine pride may be offered as explanations today, evidence suggests that the ancients, far from being credulous fools, were keen observers of the phenomena about them. Aside from the belief about the menstruous woman taming storms and whirlwinds, they continue to amaze with observations that are substantiated two or three millennia later.

Scientific Corroboration

Biblical insights into the toxic nature of menstrual blood were corroborated in a series of controlled laboratory experiments at Johns Hopkins University in 1923 by Drs. David Macht and Dorothy Lubin of the Pharmacological Laboratory of Johns Hopkins.[259] Seedlings of *Lupinus albus* were placed in a solution mixed with clean, fresh saliva from a non-menstruous woman. When the roots of these seedlings were measured, they showed little deleterious effects. But saliva obtained from the same subject at the beginning of her menstrual period was sufficiently toxic to adversely affect the growth of the seedlings. From this experiment, they learned that "the saliva, as well as other secretions studied, was much more toxic on the first day of menstruation or on the day before the onset of the same than during the later days of catamenia."[260] Tests of the blood of menstruating women revealed some samples to be much more toxic than others: red cells more toxic than blood serum, and whole blood more toxic than either serum or red blood corpuscles alone. Such toxicity produced stumpy, deformed roots of seedlings as well as growth inhibition. Further experiments with the dry blood of a menstruating woman showed it to retain its toxic properties; and experiments performed with the urine, milk, tears, and the breath of menstruating women yielded similar results.[261]

Noteworthy was the toxic effect of sweat. The high content of menotoxin (menstrual toxin) in perspiration became evident when cut flowers, such as roses, carnations, and sweet peas, were handled by menstruating women. Within an hour, the perspiration on their hands caused sweet peas to change color and droop markedly. Skin secretions of menstruous women kneading bread dough so inhibited the growth of yeast that the dough did not rise as well as expected.[262] Experiments with bacteria revealed the dramatic effect menstrual blood had upon the incubation of bacteria. At the beginning, the number of colonies of bacteria was infinite; at the end of twenty-four hours, not a single colony remained. In addition, menstrual blood in open test tubes kept longer in the air without being contaminated by bacteria than normal blood, and in certain respects the immune power of blood appeared to be greater in menstruating than in nonmenstruating women.[263]

This immune power of menstrual blood was the subject of research in the late 1980s by Margie Profet, then of the Division of Biochemistry and Molecular Biology of the University of California (Berkeley). Her research led her to propose that the immunological components of menstrual blood protect a female's uterus against infection by destroying harmful bacteria that can attach to incoming sperm and ascend the female reproductive tract.[264] The study done by Macht and Lubin, now supplemented by Profet, confirms "in striking degree the empirical observations concerning a menstrual poison prevalent in folklore and handed down in classical literature."[265]

An earlier study (1979) conducted by Prof. Norman Klein and his researchers at the University of Connecticut to determine the presence and effect of toxicity in menstrual blood was broadened as a result of my inquiry into the Levitical legislation pertaining to menstruous women. I had come across the Johns Hopkins study in the course of my readings, and discussed it with Arnold Wittstein, D.V.M., who, at the time, was an undergraduate enrolled both in my independent study course in Bible and in Professor Klein's graduate seminar on rat embryos. For reasons unknown to the members of the seminar, the rat embryos grown on female blood serum were dying randomly, even though they continued to be nurtured on the same woman's blood. Wittstein, briefed on the Macht and Lubin studies, suggested in his seminar presentation that menstrual toxin in the blood might be responsible for the deaths of the rat embryos. This hypothesis led to a series of tests to ascertain the effect of menstrual blood on the development of rat embryos in the laboratory. The tests confirmed what had been suspected:

1. Abnormal embryo growth within any given day of the menstrual cycle ranged from massive embryo death to only minor changes in the normal developmental pattern.

2. Frequent death and extreme physical malformation attended those embryos nurtured on blood drawn on the first and second days of the menstrual cycle.

3. Embryos grown on blood drawn on the eighth day of the menstrual cycle displayed almost no signs of physical malformation and looked almost as normal as those embryos nurtured on the blood of nonmenstruating women.[266]

Biblical lawmakers, knowing nothing about menstrual toxin's effect upon an animal embryo, nevertheless connected menstrual blood with human fetal development. This connection prompted them to prohibit sexual contact with the menstruous woman. Later, this same prohibition was embraced by the medieval exegete Nachmanides, who believed a child could not be formed from menstrual blood "since it is deadly poisonous."[267]

The Levitical and Deuteronomic laws quarantining a menstruating woman reflect male fear of toxicity in the touch, breath, and clothes of a menstruating woman. Thus, the hands of a sweaty menstruant will impart an unpleasant taste to food she is preparing,[268] since oxycholesterin, a steroid and a derivative of cholesterol, gets into sweat. This "contaminant" can also be spread by her sweat-absorbing garment, as when she brushes against food or people. The Deuteronomic stipulation that the non-Israelite female captive be divested of her sweaty clothing (Deut 21:11–14) attempts to eliminate any external factor that could interfere with appraising the captive's toxicity level during menstruation. The toxin (oxycholesterin) in her nails and perspiration-drenched hair required that her head be closely cropped and her nails pared. Only after these precautions are taken can her Israelite husband gauge the level of danger he will be exposed to during her menstrual period. If he were to determine she is not "safe" to live with, he must declare the marriage void and set her free.

Pliny's observation of a menstruating woman's effect on metal no longer mystifies. The "dimming" and rusting phenomena resulting from a menstruating woman's contact with the bright surface of metal mirrors and with bronze and iron objects probably are related to "the brass-ring sign," those black stains that appear under gold rings worn by women a day or so before and during the first day or two of the menstrual period.[269] The same compound that oxidizes copper produces the blood-red rust spots of oxidizing iron, and this oxidation, caused by the microscopically tiny droplets of oxycholesterin saliva in one's breath, would account for Pliny's "dimming."

Despite criticism by evolutionary biologists, Margie Profet maintained that the purpose of toxins in the blood of a menstruating woman is to protect her against sperm-carrying disease: a component of menstrual blood entering the uterus destroys a wide spectrum of pathogens entering the reproductive tract of sexually active females.[270]

The Toxicity of Childbirth

Just how closely the ancients observed toxicity in women may be judged by the Levitical law prescribing how many days of uncleanness and purification are required of the mother giving birth to a boy and the mother giving birth to a girl: "When a woman at childbirth bears a male, she shall be unclean seven days; she shall be unclean as at the time of her menstrual infirmity—on the eighth day the flesh of his foreskin shall be circumcised—she shall remain in a state of blood purification for thirty-three days: she shall not touch any consecrated thing, nor enter the sanctuary until her period of purification is completed. If she bears a female, she shall be unclean two weeks as during her menstruation, and she shall remain in a state of blood purification for sixty-six days" (Lev 12:2–5, NJPS).

This danger period requiring purification from the uncleanness of giving birth was investigated more than two millennia later by Dr. David Macht with the cooperation of the patients of the Lying-In Department of the Women's Clinic, Johns Hopkins Hospital. During a routine procedure that required every mother to return for a complete examination six weeks after the birth of her child, Macht obtained blood samples from a total of 196 mothers six to seven weeks after delivery. Examination of these nearly two hundred postpuerperal blood samples yielded the following results:

1. Puerperal bloods are less toxic for plant protoplasm than normal human blood, due perhaps to the absence of certain toxins or protective bodies in the blood of a mother after childbirth.
2. The toxicity of puerperal blood specimens obtained from the mother after female births was greater than those obtained after male births.[271]

Macht concluded that the basis for the Levitical law prohibiting the resumption of intercourse until a definite period of time has elapsed is to prevent harm to both wife and husband. The woman is in danger of contracting a coital infection due to the absence of protective toxins. The man is made aware of the danger inherent in the relative toxicity of the postpuerperal blood conditions in the female by this emphasis upon the duration of a woman's impurity after the birth of male and female children.[272] Long before postpuerperal blood came to be associated with toxins, the Levitical and Deuteronomic legislation testify to the community's perception of the possible peril of coital activity. As a result, safeguards were instituted to protect the husband from the toxicity of the menstruous wife and from the danger of resuming sexual intercourse too quickly with his nursing wife. As if to underscore the warning to Eve, which is later restated in the form of legislation advising men to exercise caution in relating sexually with women, the menstrual period is marked by *ra*, a "telltale"[273] odor offensive to biblical man, particularly if accompanied by a profuse outpouring of perspiration.[274]

Male Toxicity and Stench

Death-bearing fruit does not play favorites: Adam also emits an offensive odor after eating the fig to acquire generativity. That the odor of Adam and his descendants is *ra*, "bad," is inferred from the post-biblical description of man as *leichah seruchah*, "a [product of] ill-smelling secretion."[275] In the rabbinic *Sayings of the Fathers*, stench is associated with the sexual act: "Aqabia ben Mahaleel said, 'Consider three things, and thou wilt not come into the hands of transgression, know whence thou camest; and wither thou are going; and before whom thou are to give account and reckoning, know whence thou camest: from a fetid drop … .'"[276]

This theme is repeated in an epigram by Palladas of Alexandria (400 CE), in which man's origin is expressed in almost identical language: "'Bethink thee, man, what way thy father wrought / In getting thee, and set thy pride at naught. / Perchance by Plato's dreamings thou'rt beguiled, / Who called thee deathless, and high heaven's child. / Thou'rt made from clay? Vain boast! That tale was told to set thy spawning in a daintier mold. Wouldst know thy source, and idle prating stop? / From lust unbridled and a filthy drop.'"[277]

This resident of Alexandria, the melting pot of religions in the ancient Mediterranean world, expressed a widespread attitude reflected in the language itself: *saunion*, the Greek word for "penis," is linked by Hesychius to *sathron*, "putrid";[278] and the Latin *virus* not only means "semen," but also "poisonous liquid" and "stench."[279]

This association between semen and poison is present as well in post-biblical Hebrew, where *eres*, "drop, fluid, especially poison," is derived from the same root as *aras*, "betrothed, engaged."[280] With betrothal a step away from sexual consummation of the union, the relationship between poison and semen is manifest in the following Hebrew words:

> *yecham*, "to be hot," "to conceive" (Piel form)
>
> *chaimah* (from the same root), "venom, poison"[281]
>
> *tsachanah*, "stench"[282]
>
> *tsachanah, tsachantah*, "effusion of semen" [283]

Moreover, the word for male genitalia, *mevushim*, rendered in Deuteronomy as "the shameful parts" or "the parts to be ashamed of,"[284] should be translated as "the malodorous parts" for two reasons: first, *bosh*, the root form of *mevushim*, is equated with the root form of "to stink" as well as "to be ashamed";[285] second, semen is described as the "fetid drop." With the malodorous man suffering the distress of shame, it is understandable why shameful parts and malodorous parts become interchangeable.

The foregoing interpretation necessitates revising the conventional translation of Genesis 2:25—"The two of them were naked, the man and his wife, yet they felt no shame" (NJPS). To state that Eve and Adam felt no shame is to ask why they should feel shame. If, as Bernard Williams reasons, "the basic experience connected with shame is that of being seen, inappropriately, by the wrong people, in the wrong condition,"[286] then the experience of shame is out of the question. There are no "wrong people," since there are no other people! Under these circumstances, walking about naked is both normal and appropriate, as nudists, protected against prying eyes, will testify.

Since Eve and Adam have not yet acquired the capacity to procreate, naked Eve and Adam do not engage in sexual intercourse. No coitus, no offensive odor. The verse thus should read: "And they were both naked, the man and his wife, yet were not malodorous (Gen 2:25)."

With *ra* as the stench of death and *tov* as the fragrance of life, the phrase "knowing good and bad" falls short as an all-encompassing term for sexual behavior. "Good" no more signifies a biblically approved code of sexual behavior than does "bad" signify the opposite. The phrase "knowing good and bad," therefore, should be understood as an expression of sexual capability, with fluid transmitting fragrance/life and stench/death. This extraordinary tree, whose fruit triggers physical reactions in Eve and Adam that ultimately lead to their death, stands as the complement to the Tree of Perpetual Life.

7.
THE LUSTFUL CENTAUR

The Nachash as Sui Generis

The *nachash*, the creature in the garden responsible for a chain of events climaxing in the banishment of Eve and Adam, appears as "snake/serpent" in the translations. But from what is said—or not said—in Genesis 3, such a rendition is highly questionable, judging by the way the nachash walks upright, engages Eve in conversation, and conveys the impression of knowing God's thoughts. [287] The rabbinic sages, acquainted with ancient lore that traced the origin of the *nachash* to a primeval period when snakes walked and talked,[288] considered the snake to be an ordinary creature.[289]

Moreover, the *nachash* epitomizes craftiness, a characteristic generally associated with the fox, but snakes, observes James Kugel, are "hardly distinguished by their intelligence."[290] Such an acknowledgment of craftiness fueled speculation that the *nachash* is really Satan or Satan's agent, but identifying the *nachash* with Satan is off by about five hundred years and introduces concepts that are foreign to the text.[291] At the time of the writing of the Garden of Eden story, the Hebrew word *satan* referred solely to a human adversary. By the time Job was written (between sixth and fourth century BCE), *satan* is understood to be a member of the divine court, who roams the earth searching for human misdeeds to report to the celestial court.[292] Only later, between second century BCE and second century CE, does *satan* become Satan, the Prince of Evil, who incites rebellion against God.

Identifying the *nachash* as a snake prompts one to ask why it retains the power of speech. The text notes the snake's loss of stature, but nothing is said about depriving the snake of the ability to communicate with humans. Such a measure would prevent it from wreaking mischief again. As for the the snake having to eat dust all the days of its life, why not use the more common biblical metaphor "to *lick* the dust,"[293] if the idea is to emphasize the snake's humiliating loss of status and stature? Or, is the narrator saying that the nachash will really eat dust?

As for the origin of the *nachash*, a translation of the Hebrew using the superlative degree establishes it as being created by God:[294] "Now the serpent was the shrewdest of the entire wild beasts that the Lord God had made" (Gen 3:1, NJPS). The comparative degree, however, suggests that the *nachash*, "craftier than any wild creature that the Lord God had made," need not have been created by God.[295]

If the *nachash* is not a wild animal, is it a domesticated animal? No. Once an animal is domesticated, it loses its cunning. Like the early hominids, whose teeth and jaws were reduced in size, because they used tools to simulate these crushing organs,[296] domesticated animals no longer needed cunning so long as humans were there to protect them. The undomesticated fox, however, depends on cunning to stay alive. It stalks its prey with cunning; and employs the same cunning to escape when it becomes the hunted.

Complicating matters even further, Genesis 3:14 states that the *nachash* no longer is to associate with domesticated animals. The narrator's word order—first, domesticated animals; then, wild beasts—implies the *nachash* is more at home with domesticated animals than with wild beasts. Here is a creature more comfortable with domesticated animals, yet possessing the cunning of a wild beast. Since only humans possess these qualities, how can the story speak only of two humans in the garden, when the *nachash* speaks like a human, reasons like a human, walks like a human, and prefers the company of herbivorous animals? The answer is hybridity: the *nachash* is a hybrid with the characteristics of a human being and a domesticated animal.

Correspondence and Contrast

In certain aspects, the *nachash* in Eden resembles Enkidu, one of the main characters in the *Babylonian Gilgamesh* epic (c. 1600 BCE). The story of Enkidu begins with the nobles of Uruk appealing to Aruru, the goddess mother of Gilgamesh, to create a worthy counterpart to her son, who is two-thirds god, one-third human. As ruler of Uruk, Gilgamesh displays an unmanageable appetite for the wives and daughters of the nobles. So, to distract him from pursuing these women, the goddess-mother creates Enkidu as a companion to her son.

Enkidu, covered with shaggy hair, eats grass on all fours with the gazelles, and jostles with wild beasts at the watering-place.[297] Feeding on grass on all fours suggests the possibility that he also runs about on all fours, a phenomenon recorded about children in almost every part of the globe. But child-like Enkidu is also endowed with cunning, manifested when he foils the attempts of a trapper to catch the gazelles. The trapper asks Gilgamesh for a harlot to lure Enkidu away from the gazelles. The request is granted. When Enkidu appears at a watering hole, the harlot steps forward, disrobes, and invites him to sexually embrace her. Sated at last after six days and seven nights, Enkidu turns to rejoin his animal companions, but the gazelles, sensing his transformation, flee.[298] "The easy, natural sympathy," notes Thorkild Jacobsen, "that exists between children and animals had been Enkidu's as long as he was a child, sexually innocent. Once he has known a woman, he has made his choice: from then on, he belongs to the human race, and the animals fear him."[299] Unlike Enkidu, the biblical *nachash* is condemned to crawl on its stomach and to be isolated from all human company.

Hybrid creatures

Hybrid creatures are certainly not foreign to Scripture. In the Garden of Eden story, the hybrid *cherub*, stationed east of Eden to prevent Eve and Adam from reentering the garden (Gen 3:24), is depicted on an ivory carving with a human head and the winged body of an ox or lion.[300] Other hybrids mentioned in Scripture are *se-irim*, *serafim*, and *nefilim*. The demonic *se-irim*, haunting abandoned ruins and roaming the desert, are thought to be hairy beings in the shape of he-goats, much like the satyrs in Greek mythology.[301] The fiery *serafim*, associated in Scripture with hybridity,[302] resemble griffins, creatures with the head and wings of an eagle and the body of a lion.[303] As for the *nefilim*, they are the hybrid offspring of the sexualized angels of the Garden of Eden storyand mortal women.[304,305]

Crossbreeding was a familiar abnormality in the literature of the ancient Near East.[306] By the time the Garden of Eden story was written, the hybrid man-horse must have been a familiar figure for at least a millennium. In *Enuma elish*, the Babylonian creation story from the fifteenth century BCE, one of the offspring of the divine parent Tiamat is the horse-centaur.[307] The Babylonian priest Berossus (281 BCE) relates in his Greek paraphrase of *Enuma elish* that out of the darkness and water were born men with the feet of horses and the foreparts of men.[308] Considering the strong Mesopotamian influence on the Syro-Palestinian coast,[309] the Hebrew narrator must have been familiar with this Babylonian depiction of a man-horse.

No account is given of the origin of the *nachash*, the hybrid man-horse.[310] But then again, the biblical text says nothing about the origin of the *cherubim* stationed east of Eden or the origin of the angels in Genesis 3:5. The man-horse is simply there; and, being there, it probably hears Adam repeating God's warning to Eve to stay away from the fruit of the Tree of Procreation. Assuming that the *nachash* knows that potency is acquired by eating the fruit of a particular tree and that it has tasted this fruit, it follows then that the nachash would want to engage in sexual intercourse with Eve, perhaps to be transformed into a human, like Enkidu. If this were the goal, it is never realized, because in the end the nachash loses not two, but all four legs.

Taste Test by the Nachash

The assurance by the *nachash* that Eve "shall by no means die" attests to a certainty that can come only from eating the fruit. But Eve does not rely on the word of the crafty man-horse, who can conceal a lie with insinuating sincerity. She is guided by her sense of smell. Inhaling the sweet fragrance of the fig tree, she detects no putridity. Were the *nachash* a snake, Eve most likely would have reacted negatively to its attestation; for, unlike the goose and the gander, what is good for a reptile is not necessarily good for a human. But when this attestation comes from a man-horse, who is still alive after having eaten the fruit, its endorsement cannot be easily brushed aside. "Alive" is perhaps too tame a word to describe the man-horse at that moment. Though the man-horse/centaur may have eaten the fig to assure Eve the fruit can be eaten without suffering any ill effects, its assurance cannot conceal the immediate effect of sexual arousal. Before Eve stands a sexually aroused man-horse.

The Sexual Component of Nachash

The very word *nachash* personifies sexuality, judging by the words related to it. There is *nechoshet*, a derivative used by Ezekiel to decry the depravity of Jerusalem: "'Because thy filthiness was poured out, and thy nakedness uncovered through thy harlotries with thy lovers ...'" (Ezek 16:36, JPS). "Filthiness" is the translator's interpretation of *nechoshet*, but what precisely is meant by "filthiness" in this sexual context? To define it as "menstrual blood" is problematic, since Ezekiel uses *tumat hanidah* for menstrual blood in the very next verse.[311] Furthermore, the pouring out of menstrual blood does not accord with what the harlot does in the second half of the verse. Assuming she sets about to please her lovers by disrobing and displaying her naked body preliminary to coitus, the net effect would be to stifle their sexual urge upon their seeing or imagining menstrual blood. Lust could easily turn to loathing.

On the other hand, defining *nechoshet* as "vaginal flow" makes excellent sense. The harlot, erotically aroused, secretes so much lubricant of the accessory sex glands that she wets her undergarments even before coitus. Research has determined that "getting wet" is the automatic physiological response of a woman's body to a sexual cue in her environment,[312] thus supporting the translation of *nechoshet* as vaginal lubrication.[313] With this word, Ezekiel portrays the harlot Jerusalem as so sexually stimulated that her vaginal lubricant literally pours out of her.

The Hebrew Nachash and the Greek Centaur

The Hebrew man-horse and the centaur of Greek myth, both half-human and half-equine, differ in one major respect: visibility of genitalia. From a vase (sixth century BCE) depicting the centaur Nessos carrying the wife of Herakles across the river, the centaur has the body of a horse and the torso of a person without visible genitalia.[314] However, an eighth-century BCE bronze from the Near East shows the human and equine parts joined differently:[315] the hindquarters of a horse are appended to the small of the back of a fully visible naked man.[316] A similar figure with human genitalia in full view was found on a seventh-century BCE shard from the island of Rhodes.[317] By the time of the vase painting of Nessos, the male genitalia had been replaced by the entire equine part of the centaur, which for the Greeks embodied sexual energy. The Greeks also associated the wild male sexuality of the horse with Poseidon, who, as Hippios, god of horses, is the god of male sexuality and fertility.[318] On another Greek vase, the depiction of the neck and head of a horse as a sinuous human penis graphically equates the horse with sexuality.[319] (In psychoanalytic literature the phallic nature of the horse's neck is a recurrent dream and fantasy.)[320]

In India, lustful sexuality also is associated with the horse. Here the Gandharvas, as "The Musicians of the Court of Indra," cast their masculine spell over women by music, wealth, or pure sensuality, as manifest in the figure of bounding man-horses.[321] This lustful sexuality also appears in

Hebrew Scripture, when Jeremiah equates lust with stallions: "They were well-fed, lusty stallions, each neighing at another's wife" (Jer 5:8, NJPS).

These examples associating the horse with exuberant male sexuality in the east Mediterranean world[322] explain why the half-human, half-equine nachash expresses lustful sexuality.

Proof of Deathlessness

Eve, gazing upon the sexually aroused man-horse, knows the fig to be everything it is supposed to be, for the nachash, galvanized by sexual potency and desire, exhibits a lecherous readiness.[323] Moreover, the man-horse, very much alive, confirms the truth of its assurance to Eve that she will not die. The man-horse says nothing to Adam about the fruit of the Tree of Procreation, knowing that Adam, were he to eat a fig, would become sexually aroused and yearn for Eve with the same irrepressible ardor. Rashi, the medieval rabbinic exegete, interprets the *nachash* as having sexual designs on Eve, but attributes this lustful yearning to witnessing Eve and Adam engaging in sexual intercourse.

The rabbinic sages most likely omitted mention of this hybrid creature in their commentaries on Genesis 2–3 because of its religious implication. In the Greco-Roman period, the centaur was an all-too-familiar religious symbol, judging by the twenty-one times it was delineated on the ceiling tiles of the synagogue at Dura Europos, Syria (completed in 244 CE), and two other excavated synagogues. Jewish iconoclasts, inflamed by these depictions of the centaur, so defaced these ceiling tiles that archaeologists identified these creatures as centaurs only after intensive study of the tiles.[324] From this violent reaction to the display of centaurs in the synagogue, the sages must have purged from rabbinic texts any subject that veered too closely to paganism.[325]

The Barred Celestials

Prior to the man-horse's failure to engage in sexual intercourse with Eve, certain members of the heavenly entourage become sexualized upon descending to earth. The man-horse recognizes their sexualization by describing them as those "who know good and bad,"[326] a phrase synonymous with the possession of procreative power. These demigods, who must have eaten the fruit of the Tree of Procreation, then engage in sex. The *nachash* tells Eve about these sexualized celestial beings, who do not die after coitus, to assure her that death does not result from coitus.

God alludes to the wantonness of these celestial beings in barring Adam from the garden: "And the Lord God said, 'Now that the man has become like one of us, knowing good and bad, what if he should stretch out his hand and take also from the tree of life and eat, and live forever!'" (Gen 3:22, NJPS). In this translation *mimenu* is rendered as "of us," but this would mean that God, as a member of the heavenly host "knowing good and bad," would also have been sexualized. However, by rendering *mimenu* as "from us" instead of "of us,"[327] God is saying that sexualized Adam is like one of the sexualized divinities who are barred *mimenu*, "from us." Banished from their heavenly domain, these sexualized demigods have no choice but to remain in the garden below.

Bestiality

These barred demigods, after mating with animals, wait for the daughters of Eve to mature in sufficient numbers before engaging in sexual intercourse with them. The offspring of these unions between the sexualized demigods and the daughters of Eve are the *Nephilim*, the "depraved" or "lewd ones" of Genesis 6:4,[328] who satisfy their sexual voracity like rutting animals.[329]

The biblical world was well acquainted with bestiality. In the *Mesopotamia Gilgamesh* epic, the human Enkidu probably copulated with gazelles before taking up with the harlot—"not an improbable supposition," writes Harry

Hoffner, "since Enkidu was raised among the animals and might well have imitated the mating activities which he observed."[330] Ugaritic literature records, without objection,[331] the god Ba'al copulating with a heifer, while Hittite law splits over the issue of bestiality. The Hittites impose the death penalty on a man who copulates with a cow, a sheep, a pig, or a dog, but no offence is incurred if he has sexual relations with a horse or a mule.[332] Moral outrage is absent when the god Zeus becomes a swan to seduce Leda and then a bull to abduct Europa, but this may be explained by the Homeric Greek law that considers certain animals to be not that much more different from humans, judging by the application of the special Greek word for killing a person to the killing of an ox.[333]

Against a backdrop where the corpus of Mesopotamian law is silent regarding bestiality,[334]Hebrew Scripture stands out in its condemnation of bestiality—a denunciation connected to the Deluge. [335] In *The Drunkenness of Noah*, I argue that the purpose of the Flood is to physically cleanse the earth of the pollution caused by the insatiable sexual appetite of man, as manifested in unrestrained, voracious acts of sexual ravishing that resemble animals rutting without letup.[336] Such animal-like behavior stems from the initial sexual encounter between the banished celestial beings and the animals in the garden. One result of these bestial pairings is the birth of the *nachash*, "man-horse," who later may have fathered offspring with the same human/animal characteristics.

These offspring become even more animal-like in behavior after consuming bloody pieces of animal meat, an act that becomes habitual with the progeny of Eve and Adam. Since the soul of the animal is believed to be in its blood, the animal soul is thus absorbed into the body of a person eating a bloody piece of meat. The animal-soul then transforms the human qualities into the instincts and characteristics of the slaughtered animal,[337] a transformation that later results in prohibiting the eating of meat with the blood in it (Genesis 9:4).

With the land and its atmosphere physically polluted by successive generations of men indulging in bestiality, God acts decisively to cleanse the polluted earth. Left with no alternative, God brings on the waters of the Flood, which destroy the hybrid Nephilim and the mortal demigods in the process of restoring the polluted earth to its original beauty and fragrance.[338]

8.

DIVINE CROSS-EXAMINATION

A Mistranslation of "Nakedness"

The effect of the figs upon Eve and Adam is immediate. Sexual potency, bursting through the blockage of the sensory nerves leading to the eyes, appears as glistening wetness. Eve and Adam then cover their genitals with loincloths of fig leaves (Gen 2:25, 3:7) and conceal themselves from God. When God questions Adam regarding his whereabouts, he replies: "'… I was afraid because I was naked, so I hid'" (Gen 3:10, NJPS). Note that Adam does not say he is afraid to face God after eating the fig; rather, he is afraid to face God because he is "naked." But why does he say he is naked after covering his genitals with a loin girdle of fig leaves?

Equally perplexing is God's next question: "'Who told you that you were naked?'" (Gen 3:11, NJPS). This question implies that Adam, though aware of the sexual differences between himself and Eve (Gen 2:22–23), would not have known he is naked unless he were told. Since God does not engage in asking nonsensical questions, *eirom*, traditionally translated as "naked," means something else in its present context.

In Genesis 3:7, 10, and 11, *eirom* is to be understood as "potent." In Genesis 3:7 Eve and Adam sew fig leaves into loin girdles to enhance their newly acquired potency; in Genesis 3:10 Adam hides, because he is now potent; and in Genesis 3:11 God wants to know how Adam learned he is potent, since he cannot see the glistening wetness of potency in his own eyes.

Supporting my reading of *eirom* as "potency" in the context of Genesis 3:11 is *aram*, a cognate verbal form meaning "to make bright."[339] Eyes, bright with the sap of generativity, is the gauge by which Eve checks out the claim of the man-horse that the Tree of Procreation bestows generativity upon anyone eating its fruit. Since only the man-horse talks to Eve about a tree bestowing generativity, she looks into its eyes for confirmation. What she sees reflected in the glistening eyes of the man-horse is the clear sap of a mature fig. The fluid of life glistens in its eyes! The narrator has not stated in so many words that the man-horse has eaten a fig, but the implication is obvious, judging by its ithyphallic effect.

The Absence of Shame

Were shame the sole reason for Eve and Adam to hide from God, the narrator would have been obliged to say in Genesis 3:7 or 3:10 that shame, resulting from their newly acquired sexual awareness, forces them to hide in the brush. But the narrator says nothing of the kind, because *bosh*, as seen in *boshet*, a form of *bosh* conveying "dignity, pride, vigor,"[340] has an entirely different meaning.[341] Just as *ko-ach*, "vigor," in the sense of virility (Gen 49:3), results in a sense of dignity and pride, so also does *bosh*, a synonym of *ko-ach*, convey the same sense of virility and nobility. With *bosh* meaning "potent," a revised Genesis 2:25 reads: "The two of them were naked, the man and his wife, but they were without potency."

The root *bosh*, "potent," does not invalidate another possible translation of Genesis 2:25, namely, "malodorous." It all depends on context. With emphasis on the malodorous, *lo yitboshashu* may be rendered "were not malodorous;" and with *eirom* and *bosh* conveying the idea of potency, *lo yitboshashu* can also be translated "were without potency."

In what is the culmination[342] of an episode celebrating the dynamics of the human family, the narrator observes that a man desiring to begin his own family must separate himself from the family circle that nurtured him. Only then can he become "one flesh" (Gen 2:24) in coitus with his wife. However, Eve and Adam do not engage in sex, because they have not acquired procreative fluid. With *bosh* connected as well to the root form of "to stink" (chapter 6), Eve and Adam cannot be malodorous, since this would mean being endowed with procreative fluid. Whether the translation is "malodorous" or "potent," the result is the same: Eve and Adam, without the fluid of generativity, do not engage in sexual intercourse and thus avoid being malodorous.

Multiple Meanings

The narrator's audience, familiar with biblical punning, would not be confused by the use of *eirom* in two different ways in the same sentence. An example of such punning is this: "He had thirty sons, who rode on thirty burros and owned thirty boroughs ..." (Judg 10:4, NJPS). The translators of NJPS explain in a footnote that their use of "burros" and "boroughs" is to give the reader some idea of a Hebrew pun that employs *ayarim* as "donkeys" and then as "towns." Illustrations of biblical wordplay signify for Robert Alter that biblical prose writers "revel in repetition, sometimes of a stately, refrain-like sort, sometimes deployed in ingenious patterns through which different meanings of the same term are played against one another."[343]

Conflicting meanings of the same word in the *same sentence* are seen in *azav*, "leave, forsake" and "assist, strengthen."[344] Thus, in Exodus 23:5, the person who sees the ass of his enemy prostrate under its burden is told not to desert him, "thou shalt surely assist him."[345] Hebrew wordplay is also manifest in the poetry of Psalm 82, where *elohim* is both the common noun for "god(s)" and the proper noun for "God."[346] In verses 1a and 8, *elohim* refers to God, and in verses 1b and 6 it designates divine beings of a certain class.[347] Also in Psalm 82, *shafat* conveys "indictment" in verse 1 and "nefarious judgment" in verse 2.[348] Serving as the bridge between verses 1 and 2, *shafat* underscores the contrasting meanings of *elohim*: "God *judges* the gods who *rule*."[349]

More Biblical Wordplay

Janus parallelism, a particular kind of biblical wordplay, is present "when a polyseme," writes Cyrus Gordon, "parallels what precedes it with one meaning, and what follows it with a different meaning."[350] In Song of Songs 2:12, "pruning" is evoked for *zamir* by the preceding word "blossoms," while the bird's song that follows favors "music." Thus, the sentence reads: "The blossoms appear in the land, the time of *zamir* has arrived, the voice of the turtledove is heard in our land (Cant 2:12)."[351]

Just as both meanings in this verse from Song of Songs/Canticles are, according to Gordon, "simultaneously correct and intentional,"[352] so too the Janus parallelism in Genesis 49:26a means "my progenitors of old" and "mountains of old."[353] Attention to this type of wordplay in ancient Near East literature yields Ugaritic *nfsh* for "living being" and "appetite" in a single line of poetry;[354] Akkadian *ahu* as "enemy" and "friend" in a single sentence;[355] and Hebrew *damam*, which, like the English word "cleave,"[356] means "to be silent"[357] and "to wail."[358] Employing the same word with different meanings in a single verse testifies to the extraordinary stylistic talent of the Hebrew narrator. Unfortunately, this stylistic talent, observes Frank Kermode, is lost for the most part upon the English reader, because, "the language of the Bible supports, generally speaking, a rhetoric quite foreign in English, persistently and artfully repetitious and prone to untranslatable punning and wordplay—a feature far more natural to Hebrew than to English."[359]

The Disembodied Sound

Eve and Adam scurry out of sight among the trees when they hear the *kol* of God moving about the garden at the time of the evening breezes. Contrary to the older version of "the voice of the Lord God walking about in the garden" (JPS, Gen 3:8), the newer NJPS version reads: "They heard the sound of the Lord God moving about in the garden … ." In my understanding of the Hebrew Eve and Adam hear the movement of disembodied sound, not a voice walking or the sound of God stomping.

That a disembodied sound can move about on its own is a familiar concept in the Homeric epic, where parts of the self are treated as virtually separate entities.[360] Thus, soliloquy becomes dialogue, when the deserted Menelaus converses with his *thymos*, "the stuff of consciousness related to breath and blood,"[361] or when Odysseus rebukes his heart for barking like a dog at the serving maids.[362] Likewise in Hebrew Scripture *kol*, "sound," acts as a disembodied entity in the story where blind Isaac, duped by his wily son Jacob into believing that Esau stands before him, says: "'Come closer that I may feel you, my son—whether you are really my son Esau or not.' So Jacob drew close to his father Isaac, who said as he felt him, 'The voice is the voice of Jacob, but the hands are the hands of Esau.' He did not recognize him because his hands were hairy like those of his brother Esau" (Gen 27:21–23, NJPS).

Convinced that Jacob's *kol*, "voice," is hovering within hearing distance, Isaac relies on his sense of touch to identify the person standing before him. But more than the sense of touch at work, there is also Isaac's sense of smell. The overpoweringly pungent odor of the goat hides placed on Jacob's neck and arms dispels any doubts that the person before him is Esau.[363] In the context of Isaac and the disembodied *kol*, feeling is believing.

This perception of *kol* as a disembodied sound makes short shrift of the idea of an anthropomorphic Creator who "walks" in His garden.[364] Moreover, this disembodied sound functions like the *satan*, the prosecutor in the story of Job, who carries back reports of misconduct to God.[365] Aware of the presence and purpose of the *kol*, Eve and Adam hide amidst the trees to escape detection. When Adam is questioned by God about his whereabouts, he is forthright about his reason for hiding: "'I heard thy voice in the garden … '" (Gen 3:10, JPS). If Adam were to say he hears the "sound of You" (NJPS), he would be saying he hears God moving about in the garden. But the narrator is careful to state that what Adam hears moving about is a separate entity known as the *kol*, "sound/voice." In its role of investigator, the *kol* acquits itself quite well, for God knows what to ask Adam.

Following up on the report of the *kol*, God questions Adam about the fruit of the Tree of Procreation. Adam acknowledges eating the fruit but disavows responsibility for his action; it is all Eve's doing. Were it not for her, he would not have eaten the fig. God then questions Eve. Yes, she has eaten the fruit, but she denies responsibility for doing so. It is all the fault of the beguiling man-horse. This attestation sets the stage for the confrontation between God and the man-horse.

9.

FROM CENTAUR TO SEAL

The Transformation

God foils the plan of the *nachash*, "man-horse/centaur," to copulate with Eve by making it impossible for the creature to have any physical contact with her: "'Because you did this, banned shall you be from all cattle and all beasts of the field; on your belly you shall go …'" (Gen 3:14, NJPS).

Banishment! Never again will the man-horse roam where domesticated and other species of animals collect. This forced isolation, expressed by the Hebrew verb *arur* with the preposition *min/mi,* is rendered as "cursed" in various commentaries. Umberto Cassuto, for example, translates Genesis 3:14 as: "Cursed are you above all cattle, and above all the beasts of the field."[366] And Nahum Sarna's translation reads: "More cursed shall you be than all cattle and all wild beasts."[367]

E. A. Speiser, on the other hand, rejects *arur*, "cursed," as being "altogether out of place."[368] Not only does cursed serve to "misdirect," but to say the nachash also is cursed above all cattle and all the beasts of the field implies that the animal world shares in the guilt of the nachash.[369] Rendering *arur* as "banned" in the sense of banished, however, dispels the idea that the other animals are regarded as cursed. Moreover, Scripture can hardly speak of banishment when it is common knowledge that snakes, far from being isolated, are often found living in or near haunts frequented by animals. In the context of "banned, banished," there is, however, a creature that does move about on its belly and is truly isolated from all forms of terrestrial life. That creature is the seal.

The seal easily fits into the Eden story, because it is linked by its torso to the man-horse. Its rump resembles the rump of a horse, and it bears the vestiges of once having had hands and feet. Moreover, the omnipresence of the Mediterranean monk seal, now numbering five hundred or less,[370] once so heavily populated the shores and islands of the Mediterranean, Aegean, and Red Seas that seal hunting was an important activity in that region of the world.[371]

Like the gray and harbor seal, the monk seal is a member of the earless or true seal group, whose movements on land contrast markedly with such eared seals as the fur seal and sea lion. The sea lion, featured on television in circus acts, achieves a high degree of mobility by moving its longer, flexible hind limbs under its body. In contrast, the mobility of the earless seal is severely limited. To reach the beach, it must throw the line of its back into a strong curve and then pitch itself forward about a foot with each lurch, much like the movement of an inchworm with its continual bobbing up and down of the middle of its back. One observer notes that a seal uses the muscles of its body to heave itself along the stones like a clumsy snake.[372] But any further comparison with a snake ends here, for the seal still retains signs of limbs with its tail-like appendages as feet and front flippers as hands.

Even more remarkable is how the terrestrial diet of the seal conforms with God's declaration to the nachash: "'... dust you shall eat all the days of your life'" (Gen 3:14). Since it was known in the ancient Near East that snakes lived off rodents, eggs, and small vertebrates, exegetes had to interpret "eating dust" as a figure of speech, comparable to "licking the dust,"[373] which, judging by Assyrian friezes of captives, symbolizes humiliation.

But "eating dust," far from being comparable to "licking the dust," is to be taken literally. When God says that the nachash will eat *afar*, He is speaking of the rubble that consists of a mixture of gritty sand and angular fragments of rock. It is this mixture of sand and rock that is precisely what seals ingest.[374] An examination of 139 stomachs of elephant seals on the Falkland Islands revealed that eighty-four percent contained sand and stones varying from a few ounces to several pounds. Individual stones rarely exceeded an inch in diameter, though sea lions compulsively swallow stones that measure as much as three inches in diameter.[375] In one sea lion's stomach the stones weighed a total of twenty-four pounds.[376] Even pups that had not left the beach and were fasting prior to nutritional independence swallowed sand and stones.[377] It is speculated that sea lions, walruses, and seals swallow this mix of sand and small stones to relieve the hunger pangs of fasting by providing stomach muscles with bulk for contraction.[378] Whatever the reason, seals were known to ingest the small stones (*afar*) found on a beach.

The Seal in Hebrew Scripture

The *nachash* in Amos 9 and Jeremiah 46 is a seal, not a snake. In condemning the country's leadership, Amos prophesies that God will remove those marked for destruction from every place of refuge, be they members of the royal house, priests, civil administrators, or military leaders.[379] Were they to escape to the netherworld of Sheol, God will have them raised from the depths; were they to flee to the heavenly heights, God will have them brought down; were they to hide in the thick forest on Mount Carmel, God will have them returned for judgment. The parallelism supposedly ends when the corrupt leaders, hiding at the bottom of the sea, will not be brought up for judgment. Instead, God will send a snake to bite them in their hiding place at the bottom of the sea: "… if they conceal themselves from My sight at the bottom of the sea, there will I command the serpent to bite them'" (Amos 9:3b, NJPS).

Evidently justice will be served when the fugitives are left to die from snake bite on the bottom of the sea. What is problematic is the agent selected to finish off the fugitives. It cannot be the nachash mentioned by Amos, for it supposedly is a land snake that bites a man leaning against the interior wall of a house (Amos 5:19) but does not venture into the sea. Nor is Amos referring to sea snakes, because they are not to be found in the Mediterranean Sea, the Red Sea, or the Gulf of Aqaba.[380] True, there is the mythical sea serpent, but there is no need to turn to a mythological creature when on the Mediterranean shore is the seal, God's most likely agent. Once deployed to the bottom of the sea, the seal could easily retrieve the fugitives in much the same way a bull seal sinks its teeth into a female trying to escape from its harem and flings it back to where the other females are gathered.

Further confirmation that *nachash* is a seal is supported by Jeremiah 46:22, a passage describing the mauling the Egyptian army will suffer at the hands of the Babylonians. The traditional translation is puzzling: "'She shall rustle away like a snake as they come marching in force; they shall come against her with axes, like hewers of wood'" (Jer 46:22, NJPS). In a footnote, the NJPS translators admit their rendition is questionable because of the uncertainty of the meaning of the Hebrew. Contributing to this uncertainty is the fact that snakes do not have vocal chords. While the Egyptian cobra and Russell's viper make hissing sounds with their windpipes, and the saw-scale viper makes a rasping sound by rubbing its coils together,[381] a hissing cobra or a rasping viper is audible only to someone in the immediate vicinity. It certainly cannot convey the bedlam of butchery forecast by Jeremiah. The translators of the NJPS version, mindful perhaps of these facts, describe the fleeing snake as making a rustling sound. But "rustling," as in the rustling of leaves, hardly conjures up the pandemonium predicted by Jeremiah.

Jeremiah's figure of speech works only if *nachash* is a seal in a killing field, where seals are butchered by the hundreds. In all likelihood, seal hunters of the ancient east Mediterranean world employed techniques similar to those used by hunters on the Pribilof Islands of Alaska:[382] they would block off all escape routes to the sea, and then herd the seals into a broad area for slaughter. Seals, once aroused by the smell of blood, react with an uproar heard from one end of the field to the other. No other animal is rendered so helpless, no other animal is butchered so swiftly.

The shrieks and screams of the Egyptian forces being slaughtered on the battlefield, according to Jeremiah, will resemble the din of seals being butchered. The prophet's reference to the *kardom*, the type of ax or hatchet wielded by Abimelech to lop off a limb from a tree (Judg 9:48), would never be used by a warrior to attack a six-foot Russell's viper, because it offered no defense against a four-foot lunge by the snake. But this weapon, favored by the Babylonians for hand-to-hand combat,[383] is ideal for seal hunting. Holding the battle ax like a club, the attacker first strikes the seal in a vulnerable part of its head and then butchers the senseless animal with the blade end of the ax.

The Horse-Seal Association

The striking similarity between the equine part of the man-horse and the trunk of the seal substantiates the link between man-horse and seal. Take away the creature's legs, and the curvature of the seal's back can easily pass as the rump of a horse, its glossy coat like the coat of "sleek and lusty" stallions.[384] This similarity doubtlessly impressed the Paleolithic artists, whose engravings of seals were discovered in the Cosquer cave, a vast underwater cavern at Cape Morgiou, about five miles south of Marseilles. During the Upper Paleolithic period (about 30,000–10,000 BCE), the sea level fell to about four hundred feet below its present level, making easy access to the caves along the Paleolithic shore.[385] However, the subsequent melting of the continental glacial ice packs submerged these caves to a depth of about 120 feet. There they lay undisturbed for eighteen thousand years, until Henri Cosquer, a pioneer in underwater exploration, emerged into the main chamber in 1985. Subsequent explorations found individual drawings of the bison, horse, ibex, deer, and feline on its walls; but only the seal was drawn together with a horse or an ibex.[386] One drawing has the seal just inches from the nose of a horse, and in another, it is drawn within the forequarters of a horse.[387] Like the Paleolithic artists, the biblical narrator must have been equally impressed by the similarity between horse and seal, for he preserves just these equine features of the hybrid man-horse in transforming the *nachash* into a seal.

10.
THE LOCATION OF EDEN

The Persian Gulf

The narrator, eschewing the mythological in favor of a biological explanation of the sexualization of Eve and Adam, also avoids the mythological in his description of Eden. Far from picturing Eden as some fanciful utopia,[388] the narrator treats it as a geographic reality,[389] from which flows the source of four rivers—Pishon, Gihon, Tigris, and Euphrates. These four rivers become the reference point for Dora Jane Hamblin in her archaeological quest of the biblical Eden. Drawing upon the data of geology, hydrology, linguistics, and LANDSAT space images, she locates Eden under the waters of the Persian Gulf.[390] Before the sudden rise in sea level (the Flandrian Transgression, about 5000 to 4000 BCE), Eden was thought to be somewhere at the head of the Gulf. For Hamblin, the river that flows out of Eden and then divides into four branches (Gen 2:10–14), "joined and flowed through an area that was then above the level of the Gulf."[391]

The author may have located the legendary paradise of the Sumerians of Mesopotamia (third millennium BCE) or that of the pre-Sumerian people called Ubaidians.[392] But this legendary land of plenty and eternal life cannot be the Eden of Genesis because of (1) the subterranean water under Eden, (2) the geographical exit point of Eve and Adam, (3) the topographical setting of their new home, (4) the habitat of the seal, and (5) the adverse theopolitical considerations.

Water Under Eden

The narrator begins his story of Eden by describing the earth as *tohu vavohu* (Gen 1:2). David Tsumura, rejecting the usual "unformed and void," translates this phrase as "desolate and empty."[393] Amplifying upon the earth's desolation and emptiness, the narrator describes the earth's nascent state as devoid of vegetation; shrubs and wild plants that can grow without human cultivation have yet to appear for lack of rain (Gen 2:5).

The narrator then shifts his focus from the macrocosm of "earth" to the microcosm of *adamah*, that diminutive parcel of land (Gen 2:5) situated within the somewhat larger area called Eden. To translate *adamah* in the second half of Genesis 2:5 as "land"—"No man was there to till the land"[394]—suggests a wide expanse of cultivable soil on the order of the plantations of Egypt or Mesopotamia. But here the narrator speaks only of a single man, *adam,* to work the plot, whereas in the old Babylonian version of the *Atra-Hasis* epic, it speaks of "no people" being seen on earth.[395] Apparently, the narrator's mention of only one person means that the tract of land called *adamah* is just large enough for a single person to cultivate.

This plot of cultivable soil is watered by an *eid* welling up[396] from the earth. While biblical translations may speak of *eid* as "mist" or "dew" (Gen 2:6), Tsumura persuasively argues that *eid* should be thought of as a flow from the subterranean water coming to the surface of the *adamah.*[397] Opinion is divided over the strength of the flow of this subterranean sweet water; but it is highly improbable that *eid*, the flow or upswell of groundwater, would be of such volume that it would split into four branches, while leaving the garden looking like a flooded rice paddy. No, the pressure of the subterranean water rising to the surface of *adamah* through a spring or springs[398] is just strong enough to work the soil without major flooding.

As for the river that "issues from Eden to water the garden, and from there it divides and becomes four branches" (Gen 2:10, NJPS), surely the narrator is not suggesting that the spring turns into a mighty flow of water. Nor is *nahar*, "river," to be regarded as a "stream,"[399] since the volume of water of a stream is not great enough to be divided into four extensive rivers. No, the narrator is saying that a large, subterranean mass of water flows under the garden, "and from there" (Gen 2:10), that is, from *under* Eden, it splits into four subterranean rivers (Gen 2:10–14), which later rise to the surface.

The ancient Mediterranean world was well acquainted with rivers flowing underground. The Greek historian Herodotus notes that the Nile rises in the west, in the Atlas Mountains, and flows underground through northern Africa until it reaches Egypt. Likewise, the Danube rises in the west, in the Pyrenees, and flows underground to the east (Book II, 33–4). Babylonians believed the Euphrates flows underground to Bahrain,[400] where archaeologists found a small stone-lined room almost three feet deep in water, which came out of a pierced stone pipe or bottomless jar standing in the center of the room. The Sumerians may have thought of the sweet subterranean waters as breaking through to the surface.[401] As for the Tigris, it actually flows underground for some distance. Since almost a third of the Earth's running water circulates underground for short or long distances,[402] the ancients were relatively well-informed, despite Herodotus's theory about the origin of the Nile and Danube.

Scriptural Wordplay

Critical to establishing the location of the garden is the question of whether it is "eastward, in Eden" (Gen 2:8, JPS) or "in Eden, in the east" (Gen 2:8, RSV, NJPS). If the latter, what is Eden east of? Cassuto, presupposing Israelite authorship of Genesis, says it is "east of the land of Israel."[403] William Albright, reading the text as "eastward, in Eden," places the garden "in the eastern part of the land of Eden, which is located in the far west."[404] Decades later, Albright suggested that the Hebrew pertains to time and, therefore, should be read as "in primeval times."[405]

The spatial and temporal meanings of these words reflect the ambiguity of Hebrew words with multiple levels of meaning.[406] For example, *zamir*, as previously noted, is "retrospectively an agricultural term and prospectively a musical term,"[407] in Song of Songs 2:12. As an agricultural term, *zamir* means "pruning," in view of the preceding "flowers;" as a musical term it means "song," in view of the succeeding "voice of the turtledove." Likewise, *chamor* in Samson's riddle (Judg 15:16) is both "ass" and "heap"; *sir* in Ecclesiastes 7:6 is both "thorn" and "cauldron";[408] and *arum*, "naked" (Gen 2:25), means "guileful, cunning" in the very next verse (Gen 3:1). These multiple levels of meaning convey both the spatial sense of location and the temporal sense of primeval time.

The Exit Point

Scholars who see a parallelism between the Garden of Eden story and earlier Mesopotamian epic literature place Eden way to the east of Israel, in the region of the Euphrates and Tigris Rivers.[409] If this location is accurate, it does not explain why the cherubs are stationed only at the eastern entrance to the garden to guard against a re-entrance by Eve and Adam. Why not station them at entrances to the north, south, and west? From the silence of the text, the topography north and south of the garden evidently is so impassable that guards are not needed to prevent reentry. Then why not station cherubs at the western end of what seemingly is a valley flanked north and south by rugged hills and ravines? Since the text says nothing about the western exit, one must conclude that if there is an egress, it opens into uninhabitable terrain.

In view of these limitations, Eden is not to be located between the Tigris and Euphrates Rivers, for nowhere do steep hills enclose a lush lowland trough, with no exit at its western end. Albright's garden "in the eastern part of the land of Eden, itself located in the far west,"[410] presents a clearly defined location, if by "the far west" he is referring to the east Mediterranean shoreline. Such an egress allows the centaur-turned-seal to make its way over sand dunes to the beach. As for Eve and Adam, they are left no alternative but to exit at the eastern end of the valley leading to the cultivable hill country.[411]

The narrator, far from describing some oasis a thousand miles to the east, is actually referring to an area with which he is thoroughly familiar. By invoking the temporal phrase "in primeval times," he brings to mind the primeval caves of Mount Carmel at the mouth of Wadi el-Mugharah (*Nakhal HaMe'arot*). Presumably, the ancient Israelites explored the Mount Carmel caves with the same curiosity that people in Greco-Roman times displayed toward vertebrate fossils.[412] The stone artifacts in these caves possibly convinced them that people once lived there as far back as the period between the expulsion of Eve and Adam and the onset of the Flood. The narrator is not implying that Eve and Adam lived in such a cave; rather he is simply drawing attention to primitives who once lived there. (Paleoarchaeologists and paleoanthropologists now estimate from skeletal remains and stone tools that *Homo sapiens* lived in these caves some eighty thousand to one hundred thousand years ago.) The fertile soil, the rainfall, the springs, the drainage, and the protection from frost and storms made the area at the foot of Mount Carmel perfect for growing fruits and vegetables—factors that are ideal for situating the Garden of Eden in a locale that later sustained the primitive dwellers of these caves. With Eden at the foot of Mount Carmel, "the breezy time of day" (Gen 3:8, NJPS) refers to sea breezes.[413] An Eden cooled by sea breezes does not get much better than that.

The Abode of God

Paradoxically, the case for situating the Garden of Eden at the base of Mount Carmel is strengthened by the Ugaritic texts that speak of the abode of El, the high god of the Canaanite pantheon. When the early Israelites settled in the Canaanite coastal region south of ancient Ugarit on the Syrian coast, they did what groups of people normally do upon entering a new environment: they linked their culture with the indigenous Canaanites.[414] This cultural assimilation is evidenced by similarities of alphabet, vocabulary, proper names, verse structure, and imagery between the West Semitic (Canaanite) texts of Ugarit and the Hebrew Bible. Indeed, so extensive was this cultural assimilation around 1200–1000 BCE that, according to Mark Smith, "Israelite culture was largely Canaanite in nature."[415]

Cultural assimilation of the Israelites extended to the point of incorporating the Ugaritic location of the divine dwelling place into the religion of Israel. The Canaanite divine abode "at the source of the rivers, amid the springs of the two oceans"[416] was accepted so unreservedly by the Israelites that half a millennium later Ezekiel would speak of this dwelling as being "in the heart of the seas" (Ezek 28:2). Ezekiel further reflects Canaanite lore by associating the divine dwelling place with a mountaintop that he calls Eden, "the garden of God."[417] This picture differs from the narrator's Eden, located at the base of Mount Carmel, for it incorporates what Frank Moore Cross calls "the mythic pattern which couples the cosmic river(s) with the Mount of God."[418] Such a pattern becomes applicable to any mountain with springs of water flowing from its base.[419] A mountain with water gushing from its base persuaded one scholar familiar with the Ugaritic text to situate the divine abode on a peak in the northern part of the Mount Lebanon range, well within Ugarit's geographical horizon.[420] However, with the destruction of this cosmopolitan center of cultural and religious thought around 1200 BCE, the divine abode no longer could be associated exclusively with Mount Lebanon.

Centuries later, Ezekiel repudiates the claim of the Canaanite prince of Tyre that the divine abode is at Tyre and that he sits "enthroned like a god in the heart of the seas." The prince claims Tyre to be the divine abode, because it has the Mediterranean Sea at its doorstep and, in the words of Shalmaneser III, King of Assyria (859–824 BCE), it has Mount Ba'ali-rasi "at the head of the sea facing Tyre."[421] Ezekiel scornfully rejected any claim that placed the abode of God anywhere but in the pre-exilic lands of ancient Israel. Like the surrounding nation states asserting the dwelling place of their god to be within their boundaries, the Israelite kings could also claim the abode of God to be within their borders. The sacred mountainous abode, depending on time, place, and milieu in the Bible,[422] has been claimed for Jerusalem, Gerizim, and Carmel; but of the three only Mount Carmel has simultaneously been acknowledged by Israelites and

Canaanites to be the dwelling place of their respective deities, Yahweh and Ba'al (1 Kgs 18). The majestic promontory of Mount Carmel jutting into the sea so impressed Iamblichus, a Syrian philosopher of the fourth century BCE, that he described it as being "sacred above all mountains." [423]

On the basis of these aforementioned topographical facts, I would locate the Garden of Eden at the base of Mount Carmel (latitude 32° 40' north, longitude 35° east).

11.
THE IDENTITY OF THE SEAL

Damage Control

The metamorphosis of the *nachash*/centaur into a seal is not a punishment. Rather it is God's way of preventing the lustful man-horse from mating with the now sexualized Eve, because the *nachash*/seal, confined to a strip of beach, is effectively prevented from contacting humans. The "Fall," commonly associated with Eve and Adam, actually describes the fate of the *nachash*: "fallen" from its upright stance, it is reduced to the lowliness of a creature that inches along the beach on its chest and stomach.

The "fallen" *nachash* exemplifies the relationship between stature and rectitude, as seen in Hebrew *yashar*,[424] "right, good, just," derived from *yashar*, "even, straight."[425] When contrasted with *avon*, "crookedness, iniquity, sin," derived from *avah*, "crooked, twisted,"[426] it displays the same relationship between stature and rectitude that prevails today in such phrases as "standing for something," "standing by someone," and "taking a stand."

The "Humanness" of the Seal

Though physically transformed into a seal, the *nachash* nevertheless retains those human characteristics that probably induced Aristotle to regard seals as being like "human beings." For example, the female seal has sexual parts, except for its genital organ, like those of a woman and bears any season of the year (*Historia Animalium* 5. 567). Oppian likewise remarks upon the humanness of the mother seal when she "takes in her arms her young cubs and goes down into the sea, glorying in her children and showing them, as it were, their fatherland" (*Halieutica* 1. 690–2). Such solicitude moved one observer to describe the mother seal as "caressing and endeavoring to quiet the object of her care with a fondness almost human."[427] This "fondness almost human" is manifest between an adult male and female seal in a series of amorous water dances, frequently punctuated by kisses that precede copulation.[428]

The "humanness" of the seal is further accentuated by its ability to simulate human sounds so closely that the wail of the gray seal has been likened to a long musical lamentation heard at an Irish wake.[429] An English newspaper reported in the 1920s that gray seals mimicked a song well enough for the person singing to be convinced that seals actually sing.[430] In this regard, Hoover, a male harbor seal reared by human caretakers in New England, was renowned for its vocal mimicry. By the time Hoover was transferred to an aquarium, it had acquired a repertoire of about twelve English words (in a New England accent, no less). Commenting on Hoover, Dr. Ronald Schusterman, research marine biologist at the Pinniped Research in Cognition and Sensory Systems program of the University of California, Santa Cruz, described Hoover as imitating "human speech at least as proficiently as any parrot I have ever heard."[431]

These similarities in speaking, mothering, and lovemaking possibly spawned the stories about Selkies, seals in human form who mate with humans. At the turn of the nineteenth century, a number of families in County Kerry, Ireland, claimed to have descended from seals.[432] This claim became the storyline for *The Secret of Roan Inish*, a film about a beautiful Selkie who is married to her Irish captor and bears him children. The occasional sighting of a mermaid in remote parts of the world has been attributed to the close resemblance seals bear to humans.[433]

The Telchines

Restricted to the rocks and beaches along the Mediterranean shoreline, the *nachash*/seal is consigned to the watery domain of baleful powers—a displacement that invites comparison with the Telchines of Greek mythology. These protean beings reveal their relationship with the malevolent forces of the underwater world in assuming the shape of a "fish" with webbed fingers.[434] The naturalists of antiquity defined a fish as an armless, legless marine creature with one continuous trunk from head to tail (Aristotle *Historia Animalium* 515b24; *Parts of Animals* 695b5). Since the seal, with its flippers of webbed fingers, answers to that description, the Telchines evidently were regarded as seals,[435] feared for an evil eye that blighted "all things by their very glance" (Ovid *Metamorphoses* 7.366).[436]

Observations made by Suetonius, the Roman historian, about the Telchines reveal an association directly applicable to the Hebrew nachash. In a work produced in Greek during the reign of Emperor Hadrian (117–138 CE), Suetonius focuses on the transformation of the Telchines as sea creatures. "'Sometimes they resemble demons, sometimes human beings and then again sometimes fish or snakes.'"[437] The "fish" with webbed fingers refers, of course, to the seal, and as it moves about on dry ground, it uses the muscles of its body "like some clumsy snake."[438]

The demonic character of the Telchines is revealed in their association with metal. The Telchines employ *metis*, a Greek term derived from the mechanics of metallurgy, to convey the idea of shimmering sheen and shifting movement,[439] as seen in the shifting windblasts from the furnace bellows and the darting flames of the hearth. With windblasts of the bellows viewed as one step away from harnessing the shifting forces of the weather, the Greeks ascribed to the Telchines the magical ability to summon clouds, rain, hail, and even snow (*Diodorus of Sicily* 5.55.3). As fabricators of the scythe of Cronus (Strabo *Geography* 14.2.7), the Telchines are prototypical of what anthropologists call the "blacksmith complex" of a tribal society. Deadly magical powers are attributed to the tribal blacksmith, whose work with metal is equated with coitus and whose molten metal is equated with flowing blood.[440]

These deadly magical powers of the "blacksmith complex" are reflected in the Hebrew word *nechoshet* (from the root *nachash*), linking the magical powers of "divination" with "bronze, copper."[441] The same connection between magic and metalworking also appears in the following Latin and English words:

> Latin *faber*, "smith"
>
> *fabre*, "skillfully, ingeniously"
>
> English "to forge," (a) "to form metal" (b) "to counterfeit, deceive"[442]

The linchpin for these diverse elements is skill, synonymous with "cunning" when exercised by the metalworking blacksmith. In the Eden story, the cunning of the beguiling nachash/centaur is connected to *nachash*, the root for "bronze, copper." Likewise, the same connection between "forging" of metals, sexuality, sorcery, and deception appears in Hebrew *charash*: (1) "to engrave in metal," (2) "to plow" (in the sense of having sexual intercourse), and (3) "to engage in sorcery."[443]

The Guileful Nachash

Eve's assertion that the *nachash* beguiled her (Gen 3:13, JPS) attests to the centaur's use of the Hebrew equivalent of Greek *metis*. Eve is victimized by a master of deception. She cannot accuse the *nachash* of lying, for its assurance that she will not instantly drop dead upon eating the fruit turns out to be true; she knows through instant maturation that she will die years later.[444]

This concealment of the fig tree's lethality highlights the similarity between the Eden story and the story of Pandora in Hesiod's *Theogony*. Greek mythology's first woman, outwardly beautiful but pernicious within, is a "carrier."[445] She introduces the cycle of age, disease, and death. Man learns of her real nature only after he accepts her, but by then it is too late. The same may be said of the fig. So taken is Eve with the beauty and fragrance of the fruit of the Tree of Procreation, that only after eating its fruit does she learn of its consequences. The artfulness by which the *nachash* deceives her about the eventual lethality of this fragrant fruit matches the deviousness and treachery of the Greek Telchines.

The Shared Association with Death

The seal and the Telchines complement one another in their close association with death. The Telchines shower destructiveness upon animals and plants by pouring upon them a deadly mixture of sulfur and water of the Styx (Strabo *Geography* 14.2.7). The *nachash*/seal, as a creature of the sea, manifests deadliness by odor, domain, and equine background.

The *nachash*/seal symbolizes destruction by its offensive odor, a noisome smell of an abyss that confirms its chthonic nature. In the *Odyssey*, the "pernicious smell" of seals is so overwhelming that Menelaus and his three companions hiding among the seals of Proteus are provided an antidote of ambrosia that enables them to endure the smell (4.441–6). Indeed, oceanographers on the island of Guadelupe found the stench from the elephant seals lying on the beach to be so unbearable that they had all they could do to keep from vomiting.[446]

This picture of the *nachash*/seal as a denizen of the underwater realm of death is highlighted in an Irish legend that connects seals, horses, and the sea. Fifty seals are changed into horses by St. Brendan to carry their riders into the sea; later they become seals again when the horses plunge into the water.[447] The Greeks believed that the horse is the work of chthonic powers—a demonic creature, projecting an image of death, accentuates the equine character of the seal.[448] This image associating death with the horse appears in the Greek belief of Charos, the god of death, who rides away to seize his intended victim.[449]

The seal, with its evil eye revealing its misanthropic nature, is the perfect ally of the Canaanite god Mot, "Death." Mot, demoted from god to demon in Israelite consciousness,[450] lives beneath the sea,[451] where he and his coterie feed on mire in the gloomy netherworld.[452] The description of a netherworld of excrement and urine derives from the episode of the drunken Ugaritic god who falls into excrement and urine and is thus likened to those who descend to the netherworld.[453] Capping off this association of the *nachash*/seal with the netherworld is the creature's diet of gravel and sand, which conforms with the Greek and Mesopotamian belief that dirt is a dietary staple in Mot's netherworld.

Attack and Counterattack

The second part of God's pronouncement against the *nachash*/seal acknowledges this connection with Mot, the demon Death: "'I will put enmity between you and the woman, and between your offspring and hers; they shall strike at your head, and you shall strike at their heel'" (Gen 3:15, NJPS).

Deadly violence will flare between the *nachash*/seal and the offspring of Eve, as expressed by *eivah*, "enmity."[454] No quarter will be given by these two combatants, as inferred from the verb *shuf*, "to bruise, strike, attack," a word describing the battering a person suffers from a storm of ferocious velocity. With the combative fierceness of carnivores, the *nachash*/seal will retaliate by lunging at its attacker with the savagery of a bull seal lunging at the shoulder or foreflipper of another bull intruding into his breeding area. The tremendous punishing power inflicted by a seal's chest and neck muscles may be gauged by the way a bull seizes an escaping female with his teeth and tosses her back into his harem. In this fight-to-the-finish, the struggle between man and seal will be brutal: several hundred pounds of seal lunging at a man's heel versus a club-wielding attacker. Apparently, targeting the heel has not changed over two millennia, judging by the warning of a marine biologist who cautioned seal spotters not to get cozy with harbor seals on the beach of Montauk, Long Island: "'Get within a certain range and they'll establish that you should back off by taking a chunk out of your heel.'"[455]

Biblical Intolerance of Sorcery

This murderous assault upon the *nachash*/seal is sanctioned by Scripture's treatment of the sorcerer: "'Let no one be found among you … a soothsayer, a diviner, a sorcerer …'" (Deut 18:10, NJPS). If a person is found engaging in necromancy, that person is condemned to death: "'A man or a woman that divineth by a ghost or a familiar spirit shall surely be put to death; they shall stone them with stones; their blood shall be upon them'" (Lev 20:27, JPS).

The campaign against necromancy was relentless, judging by the reaction of the woman of En-dor to Saul's request that she bring up Samuel's ghost from the netherworld. On the night before the fateful battle with the Philistines, a disguised Saul goes to a woman reputed to foretell the future by consulting with ghosts and asks that she communicate with the netherworld. Fearfully, the woman replies: "'You know what Saul has done, how he has banned [the use of] ghosts and familiar spirits in the land. So why are you laying a trap for me, to get me killed?'" (1 Sam 28:9, NJPS). Though no specific act connects the *nachash*/seal with sorcery in the Garden of Eden story, nevertheless a connection with wizardry is implied in the verbal form of *nachash*: "to practice divination." This linkage with divination, when combined with the other negatives, is enough to condemn the *nachash*/seal to death.

The Mortality of the Nachash

The mortality of the *nachash* is inferred from the reference to its days on earth: "'… upon thy belly thou shalt go, and dust thou shalt eat all the days of thy life'" (Gen 3:14, JPS). "All the days of thy life," as with Adam (Gen 3:17), means that the life of the *nachash* will end at some point in time.

Those who recoil from pictures of hunters clubbing seals in the Arctic may find it hard to believe that the seal was regarded as evil incarnate in the ancient east Mediterranean world. Compassion for the seal would have been incomprehensible to the ancient Greek, whose fearful hatred of the seal attests to an almost total lack of representation of the seal in the Greek world. A search for reproductions of artifacts depicting the seal produced only one. On a water jar of the Greek Archaic period (c. 660–480 BCE) a seal, two dolphins, and an octopus are situated behind a giant sea serpent being attacked by Perseus. The caption of the reproduction reads: "Dolphins are not uncommon on Archaic vases, octopuses are scarce, but this seal, the Phoke, is exceptional."[456] In the cultural interchange of the east Mediterranean world, people knew the odious seal was to be abhorred. Little wonder then that this violent, malodorous creature, who is the physical counterpart of the Greek Telchines, should be regarded as an abomination to be destroyed.

12.
THE CONSEQUENCES OF SEXUALITY

Eve as Progenitor

Eve and Adam, conscious of God's warning about the lethality of the Tree of Procreation, nevertheless eat its fruit. Now they are to learn how death will enter their lives.

Eve's life force will diminish each time she engages in the life-begetting act of sexual intercourse. Conception is assured when God increases her *itsavon*, her capacity for physical "exertion," and her *heirayon*, her ability to conceive. Nothing is said about God ensuring conception by increasing *itsavon* and *heirayon* or about Eve's life force being depleted through coitus. In addition to the waning of Eve's life force, God tells Eve:[457] "'I will greatly multiply thy pain and thy travail; in pain thou shalt bring forth children ..." (Gen 3:16, JPS). Adam's *itsavon* enables him to endure the backbreaking toil of working the land. Further clarification of *itsavon* in Genesis 3:16 is found in Genesis 3:17, where it speaks of Adam producing food with *itsavon*, "exertion." Eve, also a "producer," will expend her *itsavon* to ensure her own fruitfulness. Her energetic movements in coitus, corresponding to Adam's bending, lifting, and threshing will ready her womb for Adam's seed.[458]

God jump-starts the birth process by increasing Eve's *itsavon*, her capacity to exert herself in coitus, thereby ruling out any connection between *itsavon* and the pain of childbearing. As for God increasing Eve's level of pain (Gen 3:16) during the birth process, Scripture knows of no "regular" level of pain in childbirth ever having been established. By exerting her body during delivery, Eve will endure *etsev*, excruciating pain that no man ever experiences. Related philologically to *itsavon*, "exertion," *etsev* differentiates between the exertion of a woman during coitus and the stress her body sustains during delivery. Isaiah describes the ordeal of a woman delivering her child in this way: "'Now I will scream like a woman in labor, I will pant and I will gasp'" (Isa 42:14, NJPS).

The Ebbing of Eve's Life Force

God's words regarding the end of life now assume new meaning. The woman's life force will be drained away as she loses vital body fluids through sweating during sexual intercourse and labor. Kenzaburo Oe, the Japanese Nobel laureate in literature, graphically describes this loss of fluid during delivery: "But Bird's wife lay naked on a rubber mat, tightly shutting her eyes like a shot pheasant falling out of the sky, and while she moaned her pain and anxiety and expectation, her body was oozing globs of sweat."[459]

The sweating, gasping, and crying from prolonged labor can so drain the life fluid of the mother that her *nefesh*, "soul," departs from her body much like the Greek *thymos*,[460] "the stuff of consciousness,"[461] that leaves the gasping, wounded warrior on the battlefield. Rachel suffers the loss of her *nefesh*, "soul," in the act of giving birth to Benjamin on the way to Ephrath: "And it came to pass, when she was in hard labor, that the midwife said unto her: 'Fear not; for this also is a son for thee.' And it came to pass as her soul was in departing—for she died—that she called his name Ben-oni; but his father called him Benjamin" (Gen 35:17–18, JPS). Obviously, Eve does not suffer the fate of Rachel in giving birth to Cain; but, over time, she experiences a similar fate when the cumulative effects of coitus and childbearing completely drain her of her life force.

The Ebbing of Adam's Life Force

Adam's life force likewise is diminished as he struggles to sustain his family by working what has been translated as the "cursed" land east of Eden. Jeremiah clarifies the meaning of "cursed" (*arurah*) in his comparison between the cursed man and the blessed man. The cursed man is like a bush in the desert, "set in the scorched places of the wilderness, in a barren land without inhabitant" (Jer 17:5–6). The blessed man, in sharp contrast, is one who "'... shall be like a tree planted by waters, / sending forth its roots by a stream: / it does not sense the coming of heat, / its leaves are ever fresh; / it has no care in a year of drought, / it does not cease to yield fruit'" (Jer 17:8, NJPS).

Here "blessed" connotes fruitfulness and the state of being abundantly watered, while "cursed" means just the opposite: barrenness and dryness.[462] When Eve and Adam leave the garden's well-watered flora for the parched barrenness lying beyond Eden, Adam will long for gushing water as he tills the parched soil.

"Cursed," as meaning barren and dry, provides the background for God's pledge to Noah after he and his family disembark from the ark: "'Never again will I doom the world because of man, since the devisings of man's mind are evil from his youth; nor will I ever again destroy every living being, as I have done. So long as the earth endures, seedtime and harvest, cold and heat, summer and winter, day and night, shall not cease'" (Genesis 8:21–22, NJPS). Noah and his family are to work under the same trying conditions faced by Adam, but working the land will not be any more onerous than it was before the Flood.[463] By restoring the regularity and continuity of daily and seasonal change, God guarantees that "seedtime and harvest shall not cease." Removal of the "curse" from the land assures humanity that *ba-avur*, "for its sake," the climatic conditions governing the sowing of seed and the harvesting of crops will be constant and dependable, never again to be disrupted.

Sweating It Out

Coaxing the earth to yield its bounty is a new experience for Adam, for in the garden he is responsible only for "tending" (*le-avdah*, Gen 2:15) the orchard. Under ordinary circumstances, tending would have entailed reproducing date, olive, and fig trees by cuttings.[464] Planting the sucker growing from the base of the date palm, for example, reproduces the fruit of that particular palm,[465] while ripening the fruit of the fig tree (*Ficus sycamorus* L.) is hastened by gashing the figs.[466] Current pomological techniques, refined after a long history of trial and error, *leshamrah*, "preserve," in Adam's case the fecundity of fruit trees. Adam, shaded by these trees, presumably is not drenched in sweat from this sort of work, but once outside Eden, his situation changes drastically, when he must harvest crops with much *itsavon*, "exertion."

The word *itsavon* in these two consecutive verses implies that Adam's exertions, like Eve's, eventually will bring his life to an end. The words, *be-itsavon tochalenah*, "in toil shalt thou eat of it" (Gen 3:17, JPS), suggest a picture of Adam expending much of his life force clearing the land for sowing "the grains of the field" (Gen 3:18, NJPS). These grains (*eisev*), described in the cosmological creation story as "seed-bearing" (Gen 1:29, NJPS), do not grow wild, unlike the green grass of Genesis 1:30, which serves as pasturage for grazing animals.[467] Rather, the exertion expended in hoeing, planting, weeding, reaping, threshing, and grinding these cereal plants will drain Adam of much of his life force through profuse sweating. The cumulative effect of his many "drying out" episodes eventually results in Adam's death.

With the length of Adam's life determined primarily by the degree he sweats out his life force in clearing fields, planting seed, and harvesting grain, God seemingly repeats Himself in speaking to Adam about sweating: "'By the sweat of your brow shall you get bread to eat, until you return to the ground, for from it you were taken …'" (Gen 3:19, NJPS). Since God is saying that copious sweating from working the land is life-diminishing, why does He not also include the effect of sexual intercourse? The answer is that He does—in the euphemisms "bread" and "eating."

There is no mistaking the sexual connotation of "the eating of bread" in the scene between the wife of Potiphar, Pharaoh's courtier, and Joseph, who has been placed in charge of everything in Potiphar's household "save the bread which he did eat" (Gen 39:6, JPS). The sexual connotation of these words is patent in the cause-and-effect sequence of the next two verses. The sexual appeal of Joseph, who is "well-built and handsome" (Gen 39:6, NJPS), has such an effect upon Potiphar's wife that she orders Joseph to have sex with her. He refuses, because he will not violate the trust of his master, who withholds nothing from him except his wife. Rashi, the Jewish medieval exegete, concluded from this paraphrase that "bread" in Genesis 39:6 is a euphemism for Potiphar's wife.

The connection between sex and bread carries over to the baking of bread, which is equated symbolically with a pregnant woman. The leaven for fermenting a new batch of dough causes the dough to rise or swell, a process expressed in Hebrew by *se-or*, meaning "leaven" and "rising, swelling."[468] The yeast, which causes the dough to rise, parallels semen, which causes a similar "rising" or "swelling" in a woman.[469] The Hebrew word *ibur*, "bread stuff" and "pregnancy,"[470] anticipates the contemporary description of a pregnant woman as having "a bun in her oven." Hosea links the kneading of dough with a heated oven to express sexual misconduct (Hos 7:4). This symbolism of kneading dough also appears in a Talmudic reference alluding to coitus as dining on "well-kneaded bread or on bread that is not well-kneaded."[471] And in Proverbs, dining equals coitus,[472] as symbolized by the adulterous woman, who "eateth, and wipeth her mouth, and saith: 'I have done no wickedness.'" (Prov 30:20, JPS).

"Eating bread" as signifying sexual intercourse suggests that the words, *b'zei-at apechah*, "in the sweat of thy face"[473] or "by the sweat of your brow," also have a sexual connotation. First, "your face" and "your brow" are not literal translations, for *af*, the singular form of *apechah*, means "nose" or "nostril."[474] The word is read as "face"[475] and not "your nostrils," since the phrases "in the sweat of thy nose" or "in the sweat of thy nostrils" make no sense whatsoever. But translating *af* as "nose" makes perfectly good sense, once "nose" is understood to be a phallic symbol.

Art and literature have long regarded the nose as a sexual symbol.[476] Okame, the Japanese goddess of mirth, is depicted holding on to an old man's elongated nose, which resembles a penis.[477] During World War II, "Mr. Chad," the name given to the face drawn on village walls in the European theater of operations, consisted of a giant nose with two attached eyes overhanging a horizontal line representing the top of a wall. The rounded V-shape of this nose ends sideways into two circles, suggesting two eyes attached to the nose. Except for a semicircle outlining the upper part of the face, the drawing is all "nose and eyes," which for Anton Ehrenzweig represent "a thinly veiled phallic exhibitionism."[478]

In the Negev and Golan, archeologists have unearthed Chalcolithic artifacts (roughly from the end of the fourth millennium BCE) testifying to the sexual symbolism of the nose. The Negev figurines, with their elongated noses and prominent sexual characteristics, most likely served as fertility figures. Connected with fertility rites as well are two types of basalt pillar figures excavated from the Golan.[479] Those with such facial features as horns, eyes, beard, and those without horns or beard share a common characteristic: an elongated nose. The nose on one figure measures more than half the height of the pillar. Fertility cultic practice involving large noses underscore the phallic nature of the nose, particularly when the Akkadian cognate of Hebrew *af*, "nose," not only means "nose" but also the nipple of the breast and the glans of the penis.[480]

The association of nose with penis is unmistakable in one figure excavated along with thousands of other objects during the 1920s and 1930s by American and German archaeologists at Medinet Habu in Thebes, site of a mortuary temple of Pharaoh Ramses III (1182–1151 BCE).[481] The small clay head of a man was thought to be a caricature of the Pharaoh, "for it depicts a man with a crown and a ridiculously enlarged nose."[482] This artifact, far from being an object of derision, was meant to achieve the opposite effect. The royal figure with a crown and a ridiculously enlarged nose testifies to the Pharaoh's big penis, a symbol of strength and power. The artist, out of respect for his exalted ruler, substituted an enlarged nose to achieve the same effect: the large nose/penis assures the populace of the continuing fertility of the land.

The sexual symbolism of the nose also is expressed in the act of thumbing one's nose, called making a "long nose" in German, to symbolize either the penis of the one thumbing or the penis of the one to whom the thumbing is directed.[483] This illustration casts light upon Ezekiel's reference to the act of putting "the branch to the nose" (Ezek 8:17, JPS). From *z'morah*, a vine branch used in a fertility ritual and a post biblical meaning of "penis,"[484] the "branch" is understood to be a phallic symbol.[485] Men turning their backs to the God of Israel in a ceremony associating the "phallic" nose with the "branch," observes David Halperin, was for Ezekiel "a culminating atrocity, vastly worse than anything that has gone before."[486]

With the nose as a phallic symbol, *zei-ah*, "sweat," by association connotes procreative fluid. Through Ugaritic *da-at*, it is linked to the sexualized *da-at*, "knowledge," of the Tree of Procreation (Gen 2:17). The Ugaritic language has been indispensable in recovering "lost" words in Hebrew Scripture. "Lost" words are defined as rediscovered rare words or additional meanings of still other words found in Scripture.[487] Essential to this process of rediscovery is Ugarit's preservation of the Semitic phonetic system, by which one detects ancient forms of words that did not conform to words spoken in Jerusalem at the time of the writing of Scripture. In the Ugaritic phonetic system, the "d" can sound like the Hebrew "z." Thus, Ugaritic *da-at*, "sweat," which is related to Hebrew *zei-ah*, "sweat,"[488] suggests that *da-at*, "sweat," is related to Hebrew *da-at*, "knowledge." Substantiating this insight is Hebrew *yadah*, "to know," the verbal form of *da-at*, that in the "biblical" sense means to have sexual intercourse. As Greek *menos*—related to Latin *mens*, "mind"[489]—moves forward into the nose from its storehouse in the cranium as seed carrying new life,[490] so too does Ugaritic *da-at*, "sweat" or "seminal discharge"—related to Hebrew *da-at*, "knowledge"—combine mental activity with the fluid of new life as it also moves forward into the "nose."

Relevant to this connection between perspiration and seminal fluid is Hildegard's intuitive response to the sexual implications of perspiration. The abbess of the Benedictine monastery at Bingen in the last decades of the twelfth century developed a theology of sex stressing the mutuality of female and male: Eve and Adam enjoy sex that is free of lust, lying side by side while experiencing the pleasure of sex by gently perspiring. Impregnated by Adam's perspiration, Eve gives birth painlessly months later.[491]

Hildegard may have been influenced by the Hebrew narrator's choice of words in Genesis 3:19 and the Greek concept of liquid *aion*, which, as one with the cerebrospinal fluid and semen,[492] leaves the body in the form of tears, sweat, or semen. Some rabbinic sages, expounding on the theme of population increase, shared the Greek belief that this liquid "stuff of life" either melted in sexual intercourse or left the body in the form of sweat or tears. According to one sage, the Egyptians, determined to prevent Israel from multiplying, found plowing to be the one occupation that most diminishes a man's potency by turning over a man's insides to the point of exhaustion.[493] Exhausted from plowing, the man has sweated out so much of his potency that he can not beget children.

Dustin Hoffman illustrates this association between potency and sweat in an anecdote about the public's fascination with celebrities. Just after coming to New York to study acting, Hoffman attended a boxing match at the old Madison Square Garden, where, after the semifinal bout, he saw spectators touching the winner, glistening with sweat as he made his way through the crowd to his dressing room. "I noticed this one man who kept it up," said Hoffman. "He kept rubbing the sweat off the boxer's body—putting it on his own body."[494] What Hoffman assumes to be an act of celebrity worship actually reflects a vestige of the ancient belief that links sweat with semen and semen with strength: one absorbs the strength and virility of a person by rubbing his sweat on one's own skin

In summary, the Hebrew narrator, sensitive to the propriety of divine discourse, has God euphemistically describing the effects of coitus to Adam. The "bread" Adam "eats" refers to his having sex with Eve, and the "sweat" of his "nose/nostrils" refers to his seminal discharge.[495] The result will be that Adam's coital activity and his exhausting toil in the field eventually will drain his body dry of his life force.

Dry as Dust

Greek literature illustrates the correlation between loss of semen and the diminution of life. Alexander, reports Plutarch, said that sleep and sexual intercourse made him conscious of his mortality, and weariness following coitus attested to a diminution of his life force (*Alexander* 7.22.3). Democritus called the sexual act a "small apoplexy" or "small epilepsy,"[496] and Aristotle characterized sexual intercourse as "enfeebling" (*Generation of Animals* 725b6–7).

In the Middle Ages, Albertus Magnus had this to say about the cumulative effect of frequent coitus: "Too much ejaculation dries out the body because the sperm had the power of humidifying and heating. But when warmth and moisture are drawn out of the body, the system is weakened and death follows. This is why men who copulate too much and too often do not live long, for bodies drained of their natural humidity dry out and the dryness causes death."[497]

The same "health tip" was prescribed seven centuries later in a proverb of San Blas, a rural town in southeastern Spain. The typical Andalusian husband, seeing himself as being driven to an early grave in trying to satisfy the sexual desires of his wife, had these words of advice: "If you want to reach old age, keep your semen within your skin."[498] Not surprisingly, this fear over the loss of semen did not result in significantly decreasing coital frequency between the husbands and wives of San Blas.

Against this background, the end of Adam is to be expected: "'... till thou return unto the ground; for out of it wast thou taken ...'" (Gen 3:19, JPS). To speak of Adam eating bread all his life until the day he dies adds nothing to the story, but to posit repeated coital discharge as contributing to his death explains why the narrator employs the word *ad*, "until." Adam will expend his life force in toil and in coitus *until* exertion and seminal discharges finally take their toll. Drained dry of his liquid life force, Adam returns to the ground from which he was taken.

Male Veto Power

To ensure that Eve and Adam will be sexually compatible, God grants Adam control over Eve's *teshukah*, the force that prods or urges.[499] Once endowed with such control, Adam, not Eve, will decide when and how often to engage in sexual intercourse. Adam's respect for the powerful persuasiveness of Eve's *teshukah* comes to light when he blames her for giving him the fig to eat. Behind Adam's attempt to avoid responsibility by shifting blame—"... she gave me of the tree, and I ate" (Gen 3:12, NJPS)—lies the legal principle of liability. Adam's defense is that he had to eat the lethal fruit, because he could not withstand the force of Eve's *teshukah*.

In the biblical legal system, Eve's *teshukah* operates in much the same fashion as the animating force that is attributed to the head of an ax, which "flies from the wood and finds the other man."[500] The *teshukah,* as a separate entity, comes under the law governing liability. Ownership of the object causing the damage[501] is what matters most in cases of liability. Since Eve "owns" the *teshukah* that breaks down Adam's resistance, she is liable under the law of ownership for the damage caused by the *teshukah*, Adam's caving in. That he does not readily yield to Eve's *teshukah* is implied in God's indirect reference to her "persuasiveness": "To Adam He said, 'Because you heeded your wife and ate of the tree ...'" (Gen 3:17, NJPS). With "heeding" implying pressure, Adam accepts the fruit from Eve only after he has been worked over by the *teshukah*.[502]

A *teshukah* powerful enough to cause Adam to disregard God's warning is potent enough to determine the nature of Eve's conjugal relationship with her husband. It is acknowledged that a woman has sexual needs that must be satisfied, but how often? From the narrator's perspective, Adam is destined for an early grave if Eve's *teshukah* prods him into having sex whenever she feels the urge. Nor will Eve fare any better; for vaginal secretions during frequent coitus and excessive sweating during childbirth will hasten the depletion of her life-fluid as well. So, God alters their equal-status relationship by assigning control over Eve's *teshukah* to Adam. Adam now will be the one to initiate coitus when Eve's *teshukah* is combined with his. Such a biological combination enables Adam to have sex on his terms alone.

13.
DIVINE INVESTITURE

The Naming of Eve

In naming his wife "Eve," "the mother of all the living" (Gen 3:20, NJPS), Adam confirms her sexual potency by his use of the formulaic *kara sheim*, "to name." These particular words signify fecundity, as seen in God's assurance to Abraham that he will be father to a multitude of nations: "'And you shall no longer be called Abram, but your name shall be Abraham, for I make you the father of a multitude of nations. I will make you exceedingly fertile, and make nations of you; and kings shall come forth from you'" (Gen 17:5–6, NJPS). God's promise to Abraham that he will have the capacity to procreate at the advanced age of ninety-nine is also contained in the words *kara sheim*. Likewise, the prediction to the eighty-nine-year-old Sarai that she too will be fertile is contained in the formulaic *kara sheim*, "call her name": "'As for your wife Sarai, you shall not call her Sarai, but her name shall be Sarah. I will bless her; indeed, I will give you a son by her. I will bless her so that she shall give rise to nations; rulers of peoples shall issue from her'" (Gen 17:15–16, NJPS).

The use of *kara sheim* in these two name-changes is matched by an Akkadian expression for the begetting of a son or a line.[503] In the case of Jacob, his name-change at the fords of the Jabbok is the exception that proves the rule. Jacob exacts a "blessing" from the mysterious figure before releasing him at daybreak: "And he said unto him: 'What is thy name?' And he said: 'Jacob.' And he said: 'Thy name shall be called no more Jacob, but Israel'" (Gen 32:28–29, JPS). Significantly, no mention is made of Jacob's potency, because the mysterious figure uses the phrase *amar sheim*, "to say a name." This deviation from the formulaic *kara sheim* implies that the nocturnal stranger does not actually bestow the name "Israel" upon Jacob; he simply foretells what Jacob will be called. This prediction of the stranger comes to pass at Bethel, when God invokes the formulaic *kara sheim* to endow Jacob/Israel with the procreativeness to father a line of kings and nations: "'You whose name is Jacob, you shall be called Jacob no more, but Israel shall be your name.' Thus, he named him Israel. And God said to him, 'I am El Shaddai. Be fertile and increase; a nation, yea an assembly of nations, shall descend from you. Kings shall issue from your loins'" (Gen 35:10–11, NJPS).

The formulaic *kara sheim* is also invoked to mark Joseph's name-change and his subsequent elevation to vizier, the second highest position in Egypt: "Pharaoh then gave Joseph the name Zaphenath-paneah; and he gave him for a wife Asenath daughter of Poti-phera, priest of On" (Gen 41:45, NJPS). Pharaoh invokes *kara sheim* preceding the marriage of Asenath to Joseph, whose Egyptian name means "creator of life."[504] Joseph not only becomes the creator of life upon the birth of his two sons, but also the sustainer of life by storing seven years of bountiful harvests in the granaries of Egypt.

Significantly, the formulaic *kara sheim* is omitted when Adam gives a name to the woman formed from his rib: "'This one at last is bone of my bones and flesh of my flesh. This one shall be called Woman, for from man was she taken'" (Gen 2:23, NJPS). The narrator omits *sheim*, "name," the second word of the fertility formula, because Eve, not having eaten the fig, is without generativity. It is only after she eats the fig that her newly acquired fecundity is acknowledged with the formulaic *kara sheim*. Adam gives Eve the name of *Chava*, "the mother of all living" (Gen 3:20), because she will be, as Israel Eitan notes, the "'one who brings forth, or bears; a mother,' or figuratively 'one who produces.'"[505] The stage is now set for Eve to procreate in her new home east of Eden.

After-Eden Attire

Long before the byword "I have nothing to wear" became a "buy" word, Eve and Adam walk about the garden with a loincloth of fig leaves. Only after they eat the fig does God outfit them with "garments of skins" (Gen 3:21)[506] for the life they will lead after Eden. However, clothing Eve and Adam in animal skins not only contradicts the storyline of Genesis 1–3, it also ignores the social realities of the ancient east Mediterranean world.

Being clothed in the hides of wild or domestic animals would signify the introduction of death, which has been excluded thus far from the story. In the creation account of Genesis 1, death is neither mentioned nor implied. God informs the woman and man that they are to live on grains and fruit (Gen 1:29), while the carnivores, along with other land animals and birds of the sky, are given "green plants for food" (Gen 1:30). The Garden of Eden story, which serves as a flashback expansion on the events of the sixth day of Creation,[507] is a reprise on the vegetarian theme that no living creature need be killed for food. Consequently, the Hebrew word *or* means something other than "skin, hide," as suggested by the following Hebrew words related to *or*:

> *ur*, "to be exposed, bare" [508]
>
> *ma-or* (a derivative of *ur*), "nakedness, pudendum"[509]
>
> *ur*, "husk, chaff"[510]

This association between "nakedness, pudendum," and "husk, chaff" is also found in Latin and Old English:

> Latin *volva*, "wrapper, integument; womb"
>
> *uter*, "bag"; *uterus*, "belly, pouch; womb"[511]
>
> Old English *codd*, "bag; husk, cod, skin, shell"[512]

The womb/stomach in Latin and Old English has been thought of as a "sack, pouch" or "wrapper, covering."[513] The Latin for "womb" is the same for "skin" and "husk," the respective outer wrappings of body and seed. This line of association carries over into Old English, where "cod," as "husk," denotes a "scrotum," and "codpiece," an ornamental flap or bag concealing an opening in the front of men's breeches in the fifteenth or sixteenth centuries, denotes a penis. The Greek *derma*, "skin," also conveys the idea of "prepuce" and "penis."[514]

According to Levi-Strauss, the meaning of a word or idea is discovered when corresponding equivalents for it are presented from other semantic fields.[515] On the basis of its Greek, Latin, and Old English equivalents, it can be argued that Hebrew *or* in Genesis 3:21 is not the hide of an animal but rather a covering over the genitals. Therefore, the Hebrew words *kat-not or* are to be read as the garments that cover the genitalia of Eve and Adam.

Clothes, of course, do more than cover one's nakedness; they also attest to one's status, as seen in the garments given to Joseph, the favored son of Jacob, and to Tamar, the daughter of King David. The Hebrew for this item of clothing is the same word used by the narrator in Genesis 3:21—*k'tonet* (the singular of *kat-not*). The *k'tonet,* prompting immediate recognition of status, cannot have been made of animal hides, simply because hides connote humiliation, as demonstrated by the Spartans' treatment of their helots. In a move to degrade these slaves, the rulers of Sparta required that they wear hides for the "sordid and nasty appearance" they give the body.[516] Were God to clothe Eve and Adam in hides, He would be exposed to derision, for He would be identified with the sordidness and nastiness of the two people wearing hides. This concern for God's reputation is demonstrated by Moses, when he cautions against what the Egyptians would say of a deity who liberates the Hebrew slaves, only to annihilate them at Sinai (Exod 32:12).

The narrator, aware of the damage that God's reputation could suffer, clothes Eve and Adam in garments of linen. Ideal for a warm climate, the cooler, lighter linen was worn thousands of years before the Eden narrative was written. Flax was domesticated as early as nine thousand years ago in the Jordan River valley, and linen cloth, dating about eight thousand years ago, has been found in the Judean Desert of Israel.[517] In all likelihood, then, the *k'tonet* of investiture is a linen tunic, similar perhaps to the one worn by Aaron (Lev 16:4).

Outfitting Eve and Adam with tunics recalls the outfitting of Enkidu (*Gilgamesh Epic*, c. 1600 BCE), who roams naked in the company of gazelles[518] before being lured by a harlot into a sexual encounter. Shunned by the gazelles for having sex with the harlot, Enkidu formally enters society at the shepherds' camp by being clothed in a garment. He washes his hairy body, rubs himself with oil, and wears his garment like a young noble.[519]

Eve and Adam, true children of nature, are now suitably clad in linen tunics for life after Eden. In the east Mediterranean culture of the Homeric Greeks, the power granted by a deity was manifest in the clothing and adornments worn by the recipient, or by weapons and tools used by the recipient. According to Vernant, these objects were "efficacious symbols of powers held, of functions exercised."[520] Like physiognomy and insignia, clothing contributed to the identity of a person as much as a personal name.[521] Since the human body in the flower of youth was held to be an image or reflection of the divine,[522] Eve and Adam, in tunics made by God, are to be regarded as divinely commissioned agents; and since God does not distinguish between the sexes in their investiture, both agents may be said to have attained equal status.

By this act of investiture, Eve and Adam are exonerated of the offense of disobedience. Were they guilty of disobedience, they would not have been commissioned as God's agents: for such a commission would have been interpreted as a reward for disobedience. Remarkably, God not only makes the garments, but He also clothes them (Gen 3:21) in the act of investiture. Since Eve and Adam are perfectly capable of putting the tunics on by themselves, why this personal attention by God? Surely the narrator is not suggesting that this personal fitting would have God taking in a little here and letting out a little there. No, the narrator establishes the legitimacy of Eve and Adam as God's agents by highlighting their personal investiture. Created equal in status and invested as God's viziers, they now are ready to leave the garden to become the progenitors of the future kings of Israel, who will claim authority as God's agents by tracing their descent to Eve and Adam.

14.

EDEN: A MODIFIED TRANSLATION

Genesis 2:4–25

4) Such is the story of heaven and earth as they were created. When the Lord God made earth and heaven — 5) no shrub of the field being yet in the earth and no grain having yet sprouted, because the Lord God had not sent rain upon the earth and there was no human to till the soil. 6) Instead, a flow would well up from the ground to water a small parcel of land — 7) the Lord God formed man from earth and stone and breathed into his nostrils the breath of life; and so man became a living being.

8) The Lord God planted a garden in the eastern part of Eden, and placed there the man whom He had formed. 9) And out the ground God caused to grow every tree that was alluring in its dazzling brightness, yet fragrant in its edibleness, with the Tree of Life in the middle of the garden, and the fragrant/malodorous Tree of Procreation.

10) A river issues from below Eden to water the garden, and from below the waters divide and become four subterranean branches. 11) The name of the first is Pishon, the one that encompasses the whole land of Havilah, where the gold is. 12) The gold of that land is good, bdellium is there, and lapis lazuli. 13) The name of the second river is Gihon, the one that encompasses the whole land of Cush. 14) The name of the third river is Tigris, the one that flows east of Asshur; and the fourth river is the Euphrates.

15) The Lord God took the man and placed him in the garden of Eden to tend it and to preserve its fruitfulness. 16) And the Lord God directed the man, saying, "Of every tree of the garden you may eat, 17) but of the fragrant/malodorous Tree of Procreation, you should not eat of it; for on the day you eat of it, you will initiate life-draining acts ending in death.

18) The Lord God said, "It is not good for the man to be alone; I shall make him a form corresponding to his own." 19) And the Lord God formed out of the earth all the beasts of the steppe and all the birds of the sky,and brought them to the man to see what he would call them; and whatever the man called each living creature, that would be its name. 20) And the man gave names to all the cattle and to the birds of the sky and to the beasts of the steppe; but for man no corresponding form was found. 21) So, the Lord God cast a deep sleep upon the man and he slept; and He took one of his ribs and closed up the flesh at that spot. 22) And the Lord God fashioned into a woman the rib that He had taken from the man, and He brought her to the man. 23) The man said, "This one at last is bone of my bones and flesh of my flesh. This one shall be called Woman, for from man was she taken."

24) Hence a man leaves his father and mother and clings to his wife, so that they become one flesh. 25) The two of them were naked, the man and his wife, but they were without potency.

Genesis 3:1–24

1) Now the centaur was more guileful than any of the beasts of the steppe that the Lord God had made. It said to the woman, "Did God really say: You should not eat of any tree of the garden?" 2) And the woman replied to the centaur, "We can eat of the fruit of the other trees of the garden. 3) It is only about the fruit of the tree in the middle of the garden that God said: 'You should not eat of it, or tap it, lest you die.'" 4) And the centaur said to the woman, "You surely will not become mortal. 5) God knows that, as soon as you eat of it, your eyes will glisten with procreative fluid and you

will be like those divine beings who possess the capacity to procreate. 6) When the woman perceived by its fragrance that the fruit of the tree was edible and would produce a procreative fluid reflective in the eyes, and that the tree was alluring as a source of procreative fluid, she took of its fruit and ate, and she gave some to her husband also, and he ate. 7) Then the eyes of both of them were unblocked, and they perceived that they were generative, and they sewed together fig leaves and made themselves loin-girdles.

8) They heard the Lord God's disembodied sound moving about in the garden at the time of the sea breeze, and the man and his wife hid from the Lord God among the trees of the garden. 9) The Lord God called out to the man and said to him, "Where are you?" 10) He replied, "I heard Your sound in the garden; and I was afraid because I am potent, so I hid." 11) Then He said, "Who told you that you are potent? Did you eat from the tree of which I directed you not to eat?" 12) The man said, "The woman You put at my side—she gave me of the tree, and I ate." 13) And the Lord God said to the woman, "What is this you have done?" The woman replied, "The centaur beguiled me, and I ate." 14) And the Lord God said to the centaur, "Because you did this, banned shall you be from all cattle and all the beasts of the steppe, on your belly you shall crawl, and stone fragments shall you eat all the days of your life. 15) I will put enmity between you and the woman, and between your offspring and hers; they shall smash your head and you shall lunge at their heel." 16) And to the woman He said, "I will greatly increase your exertions and your conceptions; with birth pangs will you bear children. Unto your husband will be your hungering desire, and he will exercise authority through that which is yours."

17) To Adam He said, "Because you heeded your wife and ate of the tree which I warned you about, saying, 'You should not eat of it,' barren will be the ground for you; with exertion shall you eat of it all the days of your life. 18) Thorns and thistles shall it bring forth for you, and you will feed on the grains of the field. 19) By the 'sweat of your nose' will you 'eat bread,' until you return to the ground, for from it you were taken: for earth you are, and to earth you shall return."

20) The man named his wife Eve, because she was the mother of all the living. 21) And the Lord God made for Adam and his wife decorous linen tunics, and He clothed them.

22) And the Lord God said, "Now that the man has become like one from among us who is endowed with potency, what if he should stretch out his hand and take also from the Tree of Life and eat, and live forever!" 23) So, the Lord God banished him from the garden of Eden, to till the earth from which he was taken. 24) He drove out the human pair, and stationed at the eastern part of the garden of Eden the cherubim and the fiery ever-turning sword, to guard the way to the Tree of Life.

AFTERWORD

In the course of developing my ideas about the Garden of Eden Story, I have oscillated, to paraphrase Claude Levi-Strauss,[523] between doubt and hope: the doubt that comes from dealing with tenuous guidelines to an almost impenetrable past, and the hope that enough light would emerge from the past to validate my thinking "outside the box." At the very least, my unconventional perspective clears Eve of the sin of disobedience that was said to usher death into the world. But more than exoneration, she, along with Adam, are to be acclaimed as creators in their own right. They do what God could not do in creating the universe: they banish the stagnation of Eden by creating the *future* through the birth of their child.

ENDNOTES

1 August 2, 1999.

2 The definitive work on transliteration has been written by Werner Weinberg in "Transliteration and Transcription of Hebrew," 24, 25, and Table V.

3 Westermann, 276.

4 Gary Anderson 2001, 17.

5 Sheres, 13.

6 Davies, 117.

7 Death is the answer to the great famine of Ireland in the seventh century CE, when "the prominent ones of the country conceived the plan that the people should ... pray to God regarding that onerous multitude of inferior people, that he might deign to carry off a portion by some pestilence, so that by this means the rest could live more comfortably." Daube 1976, 11.

8 In this regard, Emily Wilson, interviewed on the occasion of her translation of *The Odyssey,* asserts "that it's possible to translate the same lines a hundred different times and all of them are defensible in entirely different ways." Mason 2017, 51.

9 See William Schniedewind's compelling argument for dating the introduction of the written text of biblical literature to the reign of Hezekiah in Schniedwind 2004, 17–18, 64–90.

10 Bickerman 1959, 6.

11 Schniedewind 2004, 18.

12 Ibid., 172.

13 Ibid., 19.

14 Ibid., 82.

15 Ibid., 170.

16 Ibid., 144.

17 Meyers 2013, 60.

18 Ibid.

19 See Yee 2003 and Trible 1999, 439–44. Carol Meyers, in *Rediscovering Eve,* alerts the reader to the frequent misogynistic—and misguided—interpretations of the Eden story by the rabbinic sages and church fathers.

20 Remnick, 63.

21 Yee, 66. The story projects "a malignant image of the male-female relationship and of the 'nature' of women that is still deeply imbedded in the modern psyche." Daly, 45.

22 Manga Bible, v. 1, *Names, Games, and the Long Road Trip.*

23 Bell, 66. Accounting for some of that blame are those children's stories of the nineteenth century that are a replay of Eve's disobedience and her comeuppance. Tartar, 96.

24 Gordon 1988, 294.

25 Albright 1969, 256.

26 Saenz-Badillos, 75.

27 Gordis 1945, 174.

28 D. W. Thomas 1939, 18.

29 Greenfield 1958, 204.

30 Brown 1995, vol. 1, 14.

31 Without national borders, passports, strange currencies, or other obstacles to unlimited travel in the Bronze Age, "it was natural for Greeks, like Canaanites, Anatolians, Syrians, Egyptians, Nubians, and Libyans to sail around one another's shores, exchanging goods and learning new things, marrying one another, telling tales of 'multicultural diversity' to the children." Vermeule, 143.

32 Shanks, 63.

33 Brown 1995, 14.

34 Charmé, 40.

35 McKinlay 2011, 143–44.

36 von Kellenbach, 101.

37 Brichto 1992, 13.

38 Kahler, 109.

39 Nicol, 331.

40 Stordalen 1992a, 169.

41 Cassuto, vol 1, 1961, 85.

42 Ibid., 87.

43 Ibid., 88 and Stordalen 1992a, 176.

44 Montgomery, 264.

45 BDB, 666.

46 Another example of autochthonous creation is found in the myth of Cadmus, who, after killing the sacred dragon guarding the Ismerian Spring, sows its teeth. The result is instantaneous creation; up springs the Spartoi, fully grown, earth-born warriors.

47 duBois, 86.

48 Ovid 2001, Book One, 17, lines 373–428.

49 Hillers, 105–109.

50 Ackroyd 1968, 3.

51 Speiser 1964, 16.

52 Ibid., 14.

53 Ibid., 16.

54 Pope 1965, 175.

55 Ibid., XLVI.

56 Isa 40:22.

57 Jarvis, 216–217.

58 Ibid., 259–61.

59 Hillel, 15, 123.

60 Hertz, 10.

61 In NJPS, "divine beings" is the preferred translation. Likewise, Brichto 1998, 80: "'you will be like gods knowing good and bad.'" Cassuto, in his commentary on Genesis (vol. 1, 1961, 146) presents two possible interpretations: (a) "like Divine beings" and (b) "like the Lord God." Pointing to what comes later: "Behold, the man has become Like One Of Us," the first explanation "would apparently seem the better." However, because Cassuto finds it hard to suppose that the word God "would be used in two different senses in the same verse," he prefers (b) "like the Lord God." But this is precisely what the narrator does in the course of the story, as I explain in a later chapter.

62 Slater, 142.

63 Hesiod 1914, 331.

64 Ibid., 333.

65 Neusner 1985, I, 84.

66 Ibid.

67 Ibid., 154.

68 Contra Zevit 2013, 169. "The expression, ... when not referring to actual vision ... refers figuratively to comprehension and understanding ... . Her achievement of "knowing" would occur as a somatic reflex to the swallowed fruit. Her eyes would open themselves."

69 Unlike the half-human, half-equine Greek centaur, the hindquarters of a horse are appended to the small of the back of a naked man with fully visible genitalia.

70 Helen Schungel-Straumann argues that 1 Timothy 2:14 "is quite clearly a misrepresentation" of the Hebrew text of Genesis 3 when it "suggests a sexual transgression of Eve with the serpent." Indeed, "quite a number of apocryphal texts are solely concerned with the explicit description of Eve's sin as sexual intercourse with the serpent ..." Schungel-Straumann, 60.

71 Snell, 4.

72 The exception that proves the rule is the story of Balaam, whose eyes are "opened" (*galah*) by God to the angel with a drawn sword blocking

his way (Num 22:31). Since he was not aware that he has been saved from death by the maneuvering of his ass away from the angel, it cannot be said he has been in mortal danger. Accordingly, the narrator uses *gala*, "to open the eyes," to indicate that the danger to Balaam has passed without his being subjected to any physical harm or impairment of vision.

73 Timaeus, 68.

74 Ibid., 45.

75 Od. XXIV, 315, in Lattimore 1967, 353.

76 Onians, 429.

77 Gordis 1978, 178.

78 Jastrow, 2:1208.

79 Hesiod, *Works and Days*, 586ff.

80 Kugelmann, 176.

81 The scientific community of the seventeenth and eighteenth centuries did not consider it bizarre when "reasonable scientific men, ... while empirically studying the problems of fertility, conception, and embryology, 'asserted that they had seen exceedingly minute forms of men, with arms, heads, and legs complete, inside the spermatozoa under the microscope.'" Hillman, 354.

82 Il. XXIII, 190.

83 Il. XX, 482f. and Plato, *Timaeus*, 44D.

84 Das, 391.

85 Freeman, 234.

86 Onians, 202.

87 Od. XIX, 204–209.

88 Plato, Phaedrus 251.

89 Ibid.

90 Ibid., 213.

91 Philbrick, 20.

92 Jastrow, 2:1458. *rakot/raku* as "wetness" is translated "slippery as oil" in Ps 55:22, NEB

93 Bloom and Rosenberg, 223.

94 Levin, 111.

95 Jacobsen 1976, 111. Jacobsen writes: "The power in water that makes the soil produce was thought to be of a kind with the engendering power in male semen. Sumerian does not differentiate semen and water: one word stands for both." I am indebted to David Loveman for this reference.

96 Cogan and Tadmor, 36.

97 Blinding is linked with castration in Indian mythology, the eye symbolizing the penis. O'Flaherty 1980, 100.

98 Breytenbach, 1.

99 Ibid., 2.

100 Deut 34:7; Guillaume, 25, section 2.

101 Albright 1944, 32.

102 Collins, 21–2.

103 H. H. Cohen, 92–3.

104 Kinsey 1953, 622.

105 Updike, 204.

106 E. Hess, 46, 50. Japanese comic book artists of the manga style got it right when they intuitively exaggerated the eye size of common female anime characters. I thank David Loveman for calling this fact to my attention.

107 Bulletin 70-5485-00-0, page 11.

108 Bright, 33.

109 H. H. Cohen, 26.

110 Ibid., 93.

111 Robertson, 57–8.

112 BDB, 70.

113 Jastrow, 1:136.

114 Williams, 250.

115 Dawson, 48.

116 Ibid., 57.

117 Ibid.

118 Majno, 129.

119 Ibid., 130.

120 Singer, 60.

121 Duckworth, 35.

122 May, 1:399.

123 Elsewhere in Genesis, the narrator employs *patach*, "to open," from the technical language of irrigation, to describe the opening of the heavenly windows and the "celestial sluice-gates" at the onset of the Flood.

124 Lutz, 208–9.

125 Mattern, 30.

126 Labuschagne, 365–6.

127 Geddes, 123. The inducement for historians to read anthropology applies as well to biblical exegetes, since "anthropologists can offer detailed analyses of phenomena roughly comparable to those which the historians are endeavoring to reconstruct with a good deal less evidence." K. Thomas, 12.

128 Neusner 1985, 201–2.

129 Fay 1900, 199.

130 Onians, 217.

131 Haupt 1926, 306.

132 Erotic associations with figs are present in the Greek word *sykon*, "fig," a euphemism for vagina, and in the picture of satyrs of Greek mythology resting under fig trees when not pursuing women. The fig "was thought to arouse voluptuous feelings, so much so that some scholars considered its fruit a narcotic." Duerr, 189.

133 Majno, 151–2.

134 Condit, 25.

135 Haupt 1920, 159.

136 McCartney, 65.

137 Ibid., 65–6.

138 McCartney, 66.

139 Hertz, 10.

140 Trible 1973, 40.

141 Twain, 17.

142 Gen 2:19–20.

143 Pedersen, 164.

144 Morgenstern 1919, 110.

145 Abel, 98.

146 Rabbi Joseph Soloveitchik, revered explicator of Orthodox Judaism, omits any mention of disobedience, sin, or punishment in portraying Adam as submissive, humble, and obedient. Soloveitchik, 54.

147 "God's words therefore naturally mean an imminent termination of man's life if the prohibition is disobeyed." Moberly, 4.

148 Beattie, 73. Stephen Greenblatt contributes to the painful questions prompted by this ancient story when he asks: "What kind of God would forbid his creatures to know the difference between good and evil? How would it have been possible for those creatures to obey without such knowledge?"

149 Barr 2006, 2.

150 Ibid., 22.

151 Moberly, 8.

152 Harper, 87.

153 Gopnik, 36.

154 Aiken, 82.

155 Eitan, 49.

156 Onians, 61.

157 Ibid., 62.

158 Ibid., 44.

159 Ibid., 28.

160 Ibid., 63.

161 Ibid., 48.

162 LSJ, 42.

163 Onians, 62.

164 LSJ, 2013.

165 Palache 1959, 36.

166 Jastrow, 1:366.

167 LSJ, 231.

168 Nagy, 266.

169 Giacomelli, 4.

170 Nagy, 265.

171 Dahood 1963, 18, 20–1.

172 This tree is not the only one associated with fertility in Genesis. In a section entitled "Fertility from Divine Trees," Saul Levin cites the episode at Mamre (Gen 13:18–18:1ff.) as dealing with a "weighty case of sterility." Levin, 114.

173 Engnell, 114.

174 Majno, 207.

175 Reflective of this concept is the name Yivsam, "He is sweet-scented." (1 Chr 7:2). Dahood 1982, 394.

176 Walt Whitman is said to have had the same sweet odor Plutarch ascribed to Alexander. One physician has observed that the piny, aromatic odor noticeable in certain people becomes stronger on the approach of death. McKenzie, 77.

177 Breasted, 2:80.

178 Onians, 465.

179 Lewis and Short, 1629; Thass-Thienemann 1968, 347.

180 Scott, 5:220.

181 It is possible, but highly unlikely, that Ahasuerus would have retained his spermatic vigor during the selection process with a coital technique

similar to that perfected by the Chinese emperors, who were called upon to exhibit extraordinary sexual staying power in the performance of their royal duties. Van Gulik, 131–138, 145.

182 Driver 1968, 51.

183 Burnett, 24.

184 White, 137.

185 Ibid., 103.

186 Jastrow, 2:1474.

187 Yahuda, 176–7.

188 Forbes, 3:11, 22–4.

189 Diole, 52.

190 Jastrow 2:1474.

191 H. H. Cohen, 38–40.

192 Haupt 1924, 241–2 on Judg 9:11.

193 Goodrich-Freer, 288.

194 Mackie, 51.

195 BDB, 613, s.v. *navat*; Palache, 45.

196 Palache, 45; BDB, 847, s.v. *tsuts*. Also, *chavar* (Mishnaic Hebrew), "to be bright" and "to look with gratification [of eyes]" in Jastrow, 1:439, s.v. *chavar*; and for *shaah*, "to look upon, gaze, envelope in radiance," see H. H. Cohen, 74.

197 H. H. Cohen, 74–5.

198 Ezekiel uses *mareh* as luminosity in his vision of a restored Israel. Set down on what must be Mount Zion, Ezekiel sees a man at the gate of the city "whose appearance was like the appearance of brass ..." (Ezek 40:3, JPS). Other versions forsake literalness to eliminate duplication of "appearance." Thus, (1) "... There was a man whose appearance was like bronze (RSV); (2) "... a man like a figure of bronze" (NEB); (3) "... a man who seemed to be made of bronze" (JB). Only NJPS understood the emphasis is on radiance: "... a man who shone like copper." So, a literal rendering of the text, retaining a precise meaning of *mareh* reads: "a man whose brilliance was like the brightness of brass."

199 Heidel, 68.

200 ANET, 89.

201 Zuntz, 388.

202 A. Miller, 24.

203 Haupt 1915, 72.

204 L. Thomas, 42.

205 T. Williams, 91–2.

206 Orwell, 86.

207 Cassuto, 147.

208 Brichto 1998, 80.

209 Onians, 484.

210 H. H. Cohen, 21–28.

211 BDB, 266, s.v. *zur*.

212 Condit, 62–3.

213 Fowler, 449 in Condit, 63.

214 Condit, 64.

215 Ibid.

216 Goodenough 8:138.

217 Haupt 1920, 154.

218 Gordis 1967, 280; Hos 8:2.

219 H. H. Cohen, 36–37.

220 LSJ, 861.

221 Haupt 1920, 153.

222 Joyce, 120.

223 Sophocles, *Antigone*, 410–12, in Lilja, 163.

224 Ovid, *Metamorphoses* 7.548, in Lilja, 169.

225 K. Thomas 1992, 28.

226 *The Economist*, April 4, 1992, 104.

227 Majno, 216.

228 Ibid., 217.

229 Ibid., 52.

230 Ibid., 54.

231 ANET, 95.

232 H. H. Cohen, 36–40.

233 Macht and Kunkel, 68–70.

234 Mansfield, 24.

235 H. H. Cohen, 22–8.

236 Von Rad, 80.

237 Skinner, 67.

238 Friedman, 51.

239 BDB, 741.

240 Haupt 1917, 253–4.

241 Wood 1900, 178.

242 Haupt 1917, 254.

243 The substitution of "equal to him" or "alongside him" for "helpmate" (or "helper") is an "eloquent mistranslation" of the Hebrew. Bloom, 179.

244 Palache, 47.

245 Ibid.

246 Ibid.

247 Ibid.

248 Cassuto 1961, 1:128.

249 Ibid., 126.

250 Ibid., 2:269.

251 Eve is regarded as Adam's "counterpart," who helps him as his equal and who "in her being is most closely related to him." Schottroff, 147.

252 *Works and Days* 90–2, in Pucci, 84.

253 Pucci, 88.

254 Kerenyi, 218.

255 "... at the root of Western ideologies of woman lies Pandora superimposed on Eve." Boyarin, 100.

256 Ibid., 94.

257 Ibid. Albertus Magnus, along with other medieval authorities, believed that the eye received part of the menstrual flow, thereby causing an alteration in the air, through which a harmful vapor was emitted that darkened a mirror. Women were considered dangerous after menopause, because "various excess humors no longer eliminated by menstruation now exited through the eyes." Thomasset, 65.

258 Macht and Lubin 1923, 413.

259 Ibid., 419.

260 Ibid., 423–7.

261 Ibid., 430–5.

262 Ibid., 438–41.

263 Ibid., 455.

264 Profet, 345.

265 Macht and Lubin, 461.

266 Wittstein, in a private communication.

267 Nachmanides, 3:255–6.

268 Wittstein, in a private communication.

269 Reid, 988.

270 Profet, 346.

271 Macht 1933, 259.

272 Ibid., 260.

273 Brownmiller, 194.

274 Bulkley, 48.

275 Makhsh, 6. 7, in Jasrow 2:702.

276 *Pirke Aboth* 3. 1, in Bonner, 196–7.

277 Bonner, 196.

278 Fay 1917, 216–7.

279 Lewis and Short, 1997.

280 Jastrow 1:124.

281 BDB, 404.

282 Joel 2:20; BDB, 850.

283 Jastrow 2:1273.

284 Deut 25:11; Daube 1972, 61.

285 H. H. Cohen, 37.

286 Williams, 78.

287 Cassuto 1:139. *Nachash* is not only a general word for snake, but "probably, for other large creeping things as well, which would include crocodile." Cansdale, 196.

288 Kugel, 73.

289 Cassuto, 1:140.

290 Ibid., 72.

291 Cassuto 1:139.

292 Pope 1965, 10.

293 Psa 72:9, Isa 49:23, Mic 7:17.

294 Jerusalem Bible, Anchor Bible, RSV

295 Kautzsch and Crowley, 429.

296 Fowler, *New York Times,* December 20, 1994, B5.

297 ANET 1955, 74.

298 ANET 1955, 75.

299 Jacobsen 1976, 197.

300 Pritchard 1958, 99–100.

301 Segal 1963, 230.

302 Landy 1999, 15.

303 P. Miller, 32. Mowinckel argues that fundamentally *nachash* is the same as *shachal,* which is a poetical term for "lion" as well as the name of a "wyvern," a dragon-like creature. The lion and dragon come together in the figure of the oriental griffin. Mowinckel, 98–103.

304 Gen 3:5; see note in NJPS.

305 Gen 6:4; H. H. Cohen, 42.

306 Crossbreeding between humans and animals must have been widely accepted in Europe in the 1500s, judging by portraits drawn of a colt with a man's head and a pig with the head, feet, and hands of a man. Davidson, 103, 111.

307 ANET 1955, 62.

308 Burstein, 14; Heidel, 77.

309 Greenfield 1985, 18.

310 Though Aristotle and his followers ridiculed the idea of the existence of mixed species, other Greek writers were not as skeptical. In the Roman period of Claudius (41–54 CE), officials in Arabia reported that a small herd of centaurs still roamed about in a remote mountain wilderness, and around 50 CE Claudius heard from provincial Greek authorities of the birth of a centaur in Thessaly. In 1980 Greek archaeologists were said to have discovered three centaur burials (about 1300 BCE) in Volos, Thessaly. The curator of the centaur skeleton embedded in a sandstone slab is quoted as saying that "'while Centaurs are considered by some scholars to be mythological, the discovery ... at Volos forces us to reconsider this assumption.'" Mayor, 239–41. In view of these beliefs in mixed species, particularly in the contemporary Mediterranean world, it is not a stretch to assume that the ancient Israelites were just as credulous on the subject of centaurs.

311 Koehler-Baumgartner, 610.

312 Angier, *New York Times*, September 13, 1995, E7; Arthur E. Cohen, M. D. in a private correspondence.

313 Greenberg, 285.

314 Birchall and Corbett, plate 35.

315 Bauer, 179; Crooke, 159–60.

316 Lorimer, 184; Arkurgal, 170–1.

317 Lorimer, 178. Homer regarded a centaur as a man with a horse's body and hindquarters growing out of his back. Crooke, 159–60. Medusa, in a long scaley skirt, is pictured on a Boeotian pithos of the seventh

century BCE with a horse's body growing out of her back. Schneider, 122–3.

318 C. Segal, 144–5.

319 Dover, 133; Goodenough, v. 6, pl. 201.

320 Brill, 74.

321 Alvarez, 6.

322 Ezek 23:20, David J. Halperin in a private communication.

323 According to a midrashic text, the snake seduced Eve to commit adultery with him. Boyarin, 82.

324 Goodenough 8:114.

325 Hayman, 12.

326 Note to Gen 3:5, NJPS.

327 Harper, 199, 240

328 H. H. Cohen, 46; Brettler, 46.

329 H. H. Cohen, 47.

330 Hoffner, 82.

331 Ibid.

332 Ibid.

333 Griffin, 40.

334 Hoffner, 82.

335 See Exod 22:19; Lev 18:23–30, 20:15–16; Deut 27:21.

336 Ibid., 47.

337 Ibid., 57.

338 H. H. Cohen, 52; Hendel, 22.

339 Jastrow 2:1120.

340 Tsevat 1975, 77, 85.

341 Moberly's comment on shame is instructive. "Nor, moreover, is there anything obviously bad in the new kind of vision that the man and woman now possess. Clearly the fact of their nakedness, which their eyes had looked on before (cf.2:25), is now perceived in a new way,

but their making loincloths for themselves need not be read as an action of sudden shame and confusion in any negative sense." Moberly, 8.

342 Brichto 1998, 79.

343 Alter 1996, xxvi. Biblical narrative "reveals the presence of writers who ... delighted, because after all they were writers, in pleasing cadences and surprising deflections of syntax, in complex echoing effects among words ..." Alter 1991, 19.

344 Gordis 1936, 53.

345 Ibid.

346 Brichto 1998, 15.

347 Morgenstern 1939, 34.

348 Brichto 1998, 15.

349 Handy, 56.

350 Gordon 1982, 80.

351 Rendsburg 1980, 291.

352 Gordon 1982, 80. "Evidently, true wordplay is not all that frequent: it took a skilled poet to exploit multiple meaning." Watson, 242.

353 Rendsburg 1980, 291.

354 Particularly instructive are the Ugaritic examples in Finkel, 29–58.

355 Watson, 242.

356 David J. Halperin, in a private communication.

357 BDB, 198.

358 Ibid., 199.

359 Kermode, 19.

360 Russo and Simon, 484.

361 Onians, 13.

362 Ibid.

363 Lilja, 155.

364 B. Jacob, 26.

365 Tur-Sinai 1937, 20. The comparison of *kol* with the *satan* rests upon the word *mithaleich*, "moves about," (Gen 3:8, NJPS) which describes in Job 1:7 and Job 2:2 how the *satan* roves about the earth, looking for wrongdoers. The term "walker" in the Akkadian of the Assyrians and Babylonians is used as an attribute of the "evil eye, which travels about to inflict harm, and as the designation of a male and female demon ("road walker").

366 Cassuto 1:159

367 Sarna, 27.

368 Speiser 1964, 24.

369 Ibid.

370 Simon and Geroudet, 258, 262.

371 King, 205.

372 Thomson, 128.

373 Psa 72:9, Isa 49:23, Mic 7:17; Cassuto 1:160.

374 Maxwell, 8.

375 Laws, 17.

376 Martin, 114.

377 Laws, 18.

378 Ibid.

379 Amos 9:1–4; Wolff 1977, 336.

380 Dunson, 519. Sea snakes (Pelamis platurus) are found in an area from the Indian Ocean to the Pacific coastal waters of Central America, but never in the Red Sea or the Mediterranean. The Red Sea's high salinity and high surface temperature during the summer and the Mediterranean's low temperature during the winter effectively bar the sea snake from these areas.

381 Thomas Spadaro, New England Herpatological Society, in a private communication.

382 Scheffer, 31–2.

383 Yadin, 1:11, 12, 169

384 Jer 5:8 in J. Bright, ed., *Jeremiah.*

385 Clottes, 9.

386 Ibid., 134.

387 Ibid., 98, 130, 132.

388 Amit, 43.

389 Speiser 1967, 23.

390 Hamblin 127-34.

391 Ibid., 132.

392 Ibid., 130.

393 Tsumura 1989, 34, 84.

394 Ibid., 78.

395 Ibid., 83.

396 Hasel and Hasel, 335.

397 Tsumura 1989, 106–107.

398 Margat, 16

399 Job 20:17; Pope 1965, 140.

400 Albright 1922, 25.

401 Bibby, 271–2.

402 Margat, 16.

403 Cassuto 1964, 1:108.

404 Albright 1922, 29.

405 Albright 1969, 97.

406 Bernstein, 16.

407 Raabe, 215.

408 Barr 1961, 152–3.

409 Ottosson, 179.

410 Albright 1922, 29.

411 The narrator in Genesis 1–3 lists the basic features of his world as pasturage, field crops, rain, creating a distinctive environment "charac-

teristic of the mixed economy typical of Mediterranean agricultural societies such as biblical Isael." Hiebert, 38.

412 Mayor, 5.

413 Dahood 1981, 420.

414 Herrmann, 113.

415 M. S. Smith 1990, xxii. Biblical texts once considered corrupt have been found to be sound on the basis of Ugaritic grammar and lexicography. Dahood 1962, 61.

416 Day 1994, 37.

417 Ezek 28:13–14, 16, N.J.P.S.; Mullen, 151.

418 Cross, 38.

419 Mullen, 159.

420 Naccache, 253–64. Dismissing the geographical inaccuracy of the Gihon and Pishon as "archaic geography," Day locates Eden on a mountain in Armenia. Day 2000, 30.

421 Cogan and Tadmor, 334.

422 Gordon 1965, 233.

423 W. R. Smith, 156.

424 Straus, 536–7; Thass-Thienemann 1968, 267–8.

425 Palache, 40.

426 Ibid., 53.

427 Scammon, 153.

428 Lockley 1954, 126–7.

429 Lockley 1966, 68.

430 Maxwell, 20.

431 Schusterman, in a private communication.

432 B. Jones, 319.

433 "To the fore flippers and tapering body, the seal adds its soft, appealing eyes; seals cavort and pose in much the same way mermaids are said to. Sailors have often commented on the seal's similarity to a person seen far off in the water. Even now there are occasional, apparently

earnest reports of mermaid sightings in remote parts of the world." Fleming, 92.

434 Suetonius, cited by Detienne and Vernant, 260, 273.

435 "Upon my word the seal is indeed a malignant creature." Aelian, *On the Characteristics of Animals* 3, 19.

436 The very name Telchines, derived from *thelgein*, "enchant, charm," reveal their malefic power. C. Segal 1981, 310.

437 Detienne and Vernant, 260.

438 Thomson, 128.

439 Detienne and Vernant, 11.

440 Makarius, 32, 34, 37.

441 BDB, 368.

442 Fay 1902, 202.

443 Jastrow 1:507.

444 According to Barton, Eve and Adam knew of death at the time of their creation, when human beings were endowed with the innate moral sense Abraham appealed to in trying to dissuade God from destroying Sodom. This moral sense has to have been implanted at the time of creation, since Scripture says nothing about Abraham's morality originating in a divine revelation. Barton, 1–5.

445 Pucci, 88.

446 Cousteau and Diole, 95–96.

447 Westropp, 450.

448 Detienne and Vernant, 191, 195.

449 Dietrich 1965, 131.

450 Cassuto 1961, 2:173.

451 Gaster 1944, 33, 40.

452 Ibid., 35.

453 Loewenstamm, 379.

454 Num 35:21; Ezek 25:15, 35:5.

455 Mittelbach and Crewdson, *New York Times,* March 26, 1999, B41.

456 Isler, 24.

457 "From late biblical times to the present day, citation of Genesis 3, in particular v. 16, has been the authoritative glue sealing the document of divinely-ordained female subordination, if not inferiority." C. Meyers 1993, 129.

458 For Sir Richard Burton, the physical and emotional energy expended in coitus consisted of bucking, wriggling, leg-lifting, sobbing, and moaning. Burton, vol. 5, 3118.

459 Oe, 1.

460 H. H. Cohen, 24–8.

461 Onians, 48.

462 Gen 49:25, Isa 44:3, Ezek 34:26, Psa 84:6, as cited by Onians, 492.

463 Cassuto 1964, 2:120.

464 Sauer, 39.

465 Popenoe, 207.

466 Galil, 178–9.

467 Anderson 1992, 12.

468 Jastrow 2:1505.

469 Thass-Thienemann 1968, 135.

470 Jastrow 2:1065.

471 *Babylonian Talmud,* Shabbat 62b.

472 *Babylonian Talmud,* Ketubot 13a; Ullendorff, 445.

473 KJ, JPS, RSV.

474 Harper, 127, 199.

475 Ibid., 128.

476 Jones 1938, 141. The nose reveals the bisexual nature of symbols when it is used to represent the vagina. Saul, 53–6.

477 Baynes, 119.

478 Ehrenzweig, 213–14.

479 C. Epstein, 62–8.

480 Pope 1977, 636.

481 Wilford, *New York Times*, September 21, 1993, C1.

482 Ibid., C11.

483 Fenichel 1953, 155.

484 Jastrow 1:402.

485 H. H. Cohen, 5–6.

486 Halperin, 135.

487 Kitchen 1968, 161.

488 Dahood 1962, 63.

489 Nagy, 266.

490 Giacomelli, 12, 13.

491 Miles, 103.

492 Onians, 202.

493 Braude 1972, 123.

494 Fort Lauderdale *Sun Sentinel*, January 1, 1979, 11A.

495 The close connections between the olfactory organ, the hypothalamus, which is essential for the swelling of the genitalia and orgasm, and the glands that produce sex hormones have been designated the "naso-genital alliance." Traces of this alliance are to be found in such beliefs as the size of the nose indicating degrees of virility and abnormalities of the nose caused by excessive sexual activity. Vroon, 125.

496 Entralgo, 77.

497 *De Secretis Mulierum*, in O'Faolain and Marines, 124.

498 Brandes, 225.

499 H. H. Cohen, 80. Ullendorff defines teshukah as "'lust' in the most earthy sense." Ullendorff, 428.

500 Daube 1961, 253 on Deut 19:5.

501 Ibid., 258.

502 H. H. Cohen, 81.

503 Brichto 1973, 22.

504 Speiser 1964, 314; Plaut, 399.

505 Eitan 1929, 31–2.

506 According to one explanation, God replaces the fig-leaf covering with the more serviceable garments of skin to protect Eve and Adam from the thorns and thistles growing outside the garden. Douglas, 246.

507 Brichto 1992, 16.

508 BDB, 735.

509 Ibid.

510 Jastrow 2:1058.

511 Wood 1902, 5.

512 Ibid.

513 Ibid.

514 Henderson, 115.

515 Levi-Strauss 1991, 142.

516 Vernant 1991, 233.

517 Wilford, *New York Times*, July 13, 1993, C8.

518 Jacobsen 1976, 197.

519 Ibid., 198–9.

520 Vernant 1991, 38.

521 Ibid., 47.

522 Ibid., 159.

523 Levi-Strauss 1975, 260.

BIBLIOGRAPHY

Aaron, David H. *Biblical Ambiguities: Metaphor, Semantics and Divine Imagery*. Leiden: Brill, 2001.

Abel, Carl. *Linguistic Essays*. London: Trubner, 1882.

Abraham, Karl. *Clinical Papers and Essays on Psycho-analysis*. London: Hogarth Press, 1955.

Ackerman, Diane. "Last Refuge of the Monk Seal." *National Geographic* 181 (1992): 128–44.

Ackerman, Susan. "A 'Marzeah' in Ezekiel 8:7–13?" *Harvard Theological Review* 82 (1989): 267–81.

———. "The Queen Mother and the Cult in Ancient Israel," *Journal of Biblical Literature* 112 (1993): 385–401.

Ackroyd, Peter R. "The Hebrew Root," *Journal of Theological Studies*, 2 (1951): 31–6.

———. "Meaning and Exegesis." In *Words and Meaning*, edited by P. R. Ackroyd and Barnabas Lindars, Cambridge: Cambridge Univ. Press, 1968.

———. "The Jewish Community in Palestine in the Persian Period." In *Cambridge History of Judaism*, edited by W.D. Davies and L. Finkelstein. vol. 1. Cambridge: Cambridge Univ. Press, 1984.

Adams, J. N. *The Latin Sexual Vocabulary*. Baltimore: Johns Hopkins Press, 1982.

Adkins, A. W. H. *A Study of Personality and Views of Human Nature in the Context of Ancient Greek Society, Value, and Beliefs*. Ithaca: Cornell Univ. Press, 1970.

Aelian. *On the Characteristics of Animals,* translated by A. F. Scholfield. Loeb Classical Library. Vol. 1. London: William Heinemann, 1958.

Ahlstrom, Gosta W. *The History of Ancient Palestine.* Minneapolis: Fortress Press, 1993.

Aiken, Conrad. *Preludes: Preludes for Memnon and Time in the Rock.* New York: Oxford Univ. Press (A Galaxy Book), 1966.

Akenson, Donald Harman. *Surpassing Wonder: The Invention of the Bible and the Talmuds.* Montreal: McGill-Queen's Univ. Press, 1998.

Akurgal, Ekrem. *The Art of Greece: Its Origins in the Mediterranean and Near East,* translated by Wayne Dynes. New York: Crown, 1968.

Albertz, Rainer. *A History of Israelite Religion in the Old Testament Period.* Vol. 2, translated by John Bowden. London: SCM Press, 1994.

Albright, William F. "The Location of the Garden of Eden," *American Journal of Semitic Languages* 39 (1922):15–31.

———. "The 'Natural Force' of Moses in the Light of Ugaritic," *Bulletin of the American Schools of Oriental Research* 94 (1944): 32–35.

———. *Archeology and the Religion of Israel.* Baltimore: Johns Hopkins Press, 1946a.

———. *From the Stone Age to Christianity.* Baltimore: Johns Hopkins Press, 1946b.

———.*Yahweh and the Gods of Canaan: An Historic Analysis of Two Contrasting Faiths.* New York: Anchor Books/Doubleday, 1969.

Alexander, Caroline. *The War That Killed Achilles: The True Story of Homer's* Iliad *and the Trojan War.* New York: Viking, 2009.

Alter, Robert. *The Art of Biblical Narrative.* New York: Basic Books, 1981.

———. "Biblical Imperatives and Literary Play." In *"Not in Heaven": Coherence and Complexity in Biblical Narrative,* edited by Jason P. Rosenblatt and Joseph C. Sitterson, Jr. Bloomington: Indiana Univ. Press, 1991.

———. *Genesis: A New Translation with Commentary.* New York: Norton, 1996.

———. *Ancient Israel: The Former Prophets: Joshua, Judges, Samuel and Kings: a translation and Commentary.* New York: Norton, 2013.

Alvarez, Octavio. *The Celestial Brides*. Stockbridge, MA: Herbert Reichner, 1978.

Amaru, Betsy Halpern. "The First Woman, Wives, and Mothers in Jubilees," *Journal of Biblical Literature* 113 (1994): 609–26.

Andersen, Francis I. "Biconsonantal Byforms of Weak Hebrew Roots." *Zeitschrift für die alttestamentliche Wissenschaft* 82 (1970): 270–75.

Anderson, Gary. "The Cosmic Mountain" in *Genesis 1-3 in the History of Exegesis,* edited by Gregory Allen Robbins. Lewiston, Maine: Edward Mellend Press, 1988.

———. "Celibacy or Consummation in the Garden? Reflections on Early Jewish and Christian Interpretations of the Garden of Eden." *Harvard Theological Review* 82 (1989):121–48.

———. "Biblical Origins and the Problem of the Fall." *Pro Ecclesia* 10 (2001): 1–14.

Andrewes, Antony. *The Greeks*. New York: Norton, 1978.

Angier, Natalie. "Radical New View of Role of Menstruation." *New York Times* (New York), September 21, 1993.

———. "Conversations/Ellen T.M. Laan." *New York Times* (New York), August 13, 1995.

Apocrypha and Pseudepigrapha of the Old Testament. Charles, R.H., edited by 1913. Reprint. Oxford: Clarendon Press, 1969.

Aristotle. *Parts of Animals,* translated by A. L. Peck. Loeb Classical Library. London: William Heinemann, 1937.

———. *Historia Animalium,* translated by A. L. Peck. Loeb Classical Library. Cambridge, MA: Harvard Univ. Press, 1952.

———.*Generation of Animals,* translated by A. L. Peck. Loeb Classical Library. 1943. Reprint. London: William Heinemann, 1953.

Arlow, Jacob A. "Metaphor and the Psychoanalytic Situation." *Psychoanalytic Quarterly* 48 (1979): 363–85.

Aruz, Joan, edited by *Art of the First Cities: The Third Millennium B. C. from the Mediterranean to the Indus*. New York: Metropolitan Museum of Art, 2003.

Athanassakis, Apostolos. *The Homeric Hymns*. Baltimore: Johns Hopkins Univ. Press.

Austin, M. M. 1990 "Greek Tyrants and the Persians, 546–479 B.C." *Classical Quarterly* 40 (1976): 298–306.

Avalos, Hector. *Illness and Health Care in the Ancient Near East*. Atlanta: Scholars Press, 1995.

Barclay, John. "Apologetics in the Jewish Diaspora" in *Jews in the Hellenistic and Roman Cities*," edited by John R. Bartlett, London: Routledge, 2002.

Baker, Sidney J. "Language and Dreams," *International Journal of Psychoanalysis* 31 (1950): 171–78.

Bar-Kochva, Bezalel. *Pseudo-Hecataeus, On the Jews: Legitimizing the Jewish Diaspora*. Berkeley: Univ. of California Press. 1996.

———. *The Image of the Jews in Greek Literature: The Hellenistic Period*. Berkeley: Univ. of California Press, 2010.

Bar-Yosef, Ofer and Bernard Vandermeersch. "Modern Humans in the Levant," *Scientific American* 268 (1993): 94–100.

Barker, Margaret. *The Older Testament*. London: SPCK, 1987.

Barr, James. *The Semantics of Biblical Language*. London: Oxford Univ. Press, 1961.

———. *Comparative Philology and the Text of the Old Testament*. Oxford: Clarendon Press, 1968.

———. "The Symbolism of Names in Old Testament," *Bulletin of the John Rylands University Library of Manchester* 52 (1969–70): 11–29.

———. "One Man, or All Humanity?" In *Recycling Biblical Figures*, edited by Athalya Brenner and Jan Willem van Henten. Leiden: Deo Publishing, 1999.

———. "Is God A Liar? (Genesis 2–3)—And Related Matters," *Journal of Theological Studies* 57 (2006): 1–22.

Barrick, W. Boyd. "On the Meaning of and the Composition of the Kings History." *Journal of Biblical Literature* 115 (1996): 621–42.

Barton, John. "Natural Law and Poetic Justice in the Old Testament." *Journal of Theological Studies* 30 (1979): 1–14.

———. *Reading the Old Testament*. Philadelphia: Westminster Press, 1984.

———. "Looking Back on the 20th Century: Old Testament Studies." *The Expository Times* 110 (1999): 348–51.

Bauman, Zygmunt. *Legislators and Interpreters*. Ithaca: Cornell Univ. Press, 1987.

Baur, Paul V.C. *Centaurs in Ancient Art—The Archaic Period*. Berlin: Karl Curtius, 1912.

Baynes, Ken. *Art in Society*. Woodstock, New York: Overlook Press, 1975.

Beal, Timothy. *The Rise and Fall of the Bible*. Boston: Houghton Mifflin Harcourt, 2011.

Beattie, D. R. G. "Peshat and Derash in the Garden of Eden." *Irish Biblical Studies* 7 (1985): 62–75.

Beck, Pirhiya. "The Drawings from Horvat Teiman (Kuntillet Ajrud)." *Tel Aviv* 9 (1982): 3–68.

"Bed and Breakfast—and Blessings." *Biblical Archaeological Review* 22 (1996): 12.

Bell, Rob. *Love Wins*. New York: Harper Collins, 2010.

Ben Zvi, Ehud. "Inclusion in and Exclusion from Israel as Conveyed by the Use of the Term 'Israel' in Post-Monarchic Biblical Texts." In *The Pitcher Is Broken*, edited by Steven W. Holloway and Lowell K. Handy. Sheffield: Sheffield Academic Press, 1995.

Bernstein, Moshe. "Two Multivalent Readings in Ruth." *Journal for the Study of the Old Testament* 50 (1991): 15–26.

Bibby, Geoffrey. *Looking for Dilmun*. New York: Knopf, 1969.

Bickerman, Elias J. "The Septuagint as a Translation." In *Proceedings of the American academy of Jewish Research* 28 (1959): 1–39.

———. *The Jews in the Greek Age*. Cambridge, MA: Harvard Univ. Press, 1988.

Blenkinsopp, Joseph. "The Mission of Udjahorresnet and Those of Ezra and Nehemiah." *Journal of Biblical Literature* 106 (1987): 409–21.

Bliss, Frederick Jones and R.A. Stewart Macalister. *Excavations in Palestine 1898–1900*. London: Palestine Exploration Fund, 1902.

Bloch-Smith, Elizabeth M. "The Cult of the Dead in Judah: Interpreting the Material Remains." *Journal of Biblical Literature* 111 (1992): 213–24.

Bloom, Harold and David Rosenberg. *The Book of J*. New York: Grove Weidenfeld, 1990.

Bonner, Campbell. "Palladas and Jewish Reflections upon the Beginnings of Man." *Journal of the American Oriental Society* 55 (1935): 196–99.

Borowski, Oded. "Hezekiah's Reforms and the Revolt against Assyria." *Biblical Archaeologist* 58 (1995): 148–55.

Bowra, C.M. *Early Greek Elegists*. 1938 Reprint. New York: Cooper Square Publishers, 1969.

Boyarin, Daniel. *Carnal Israel*. Berkeley: Univ. of California Press, 1993.

Brandes, Stanley. "Like Wounded Stags: Male Sexual Ideology in an Andalusian Town." In *Sexual Meanings*, edited by Sherry B. Ortner and Harriet Whitehead. Cambridge: Cambridge Univ. Press, 1981.

Braude, William G., translator and commentator. *Pesikta Rabbati*, 2 vols. New Haven: Yale Univ. Press, 1968.

Brenner, Atalya, editor. *A Feminist Companion to Genesis*. Sheffield: Scheffield Academic Press, 1993.

———. *The Intercourse of Knowledge: on gendering desire and 'sexuality' in the Hebrew Bible*. Leiden: Brill, 1997.

Brenner, Charles. *An Elementary Textbook of Psychoanalysis*. Garden City: Doubleday Anchor, 1957.

Brettler, Marc Zvi. *The Book of Judges*. London: Routledge, 2002.

Breytenbach, A. P. B. "The Connection Between the Concepts of Darkness and Drought as well as Light and Vegetation." In *De Fructu Oris Sui*, Pretoria Oriental Series, IX, Ed I. H. Eybers, F. C. Fensham, C. J. Labuschagne. Leiden: Brill, 1971.

Brichto, Herbert Chanan. "Kin, Cult, Land, and Afterlife—A Biblical Complex." *Hebrew Union College Annual* 44 (1973): 1–54.

———. "The Worship of the Golden Calf: A Literary Analysis of a Fable on Idolatry." *Hebrew Union College Annual* 54 (1983): 1–44.

———.*Toward a Grammar of Biblical Poetics: Tales of the Prophets*. New York: Oxford Univ. Press, 1992.

———.*The Names of God: Poetic Readings in Biblical Beginnings*. New York: Oxford Univ. Press, 1998.

Bright, John. *Jeremiah*. Anchor Bible. Garden City, New York: Doubleday, 1965.

Brill, A.A. "The Universality of Symbols." In *The Yearbook of Psychoanalysis*, edited by Sandor Lorand. Vol. 3. New York: International Universities Press, 1945.

Brown, F., S. R. Driver, and C. A. Briggs, eds. *A Hebrew and English Lexicon of the Old Testament*.

Brown, John Pairman. "Yahweh, Zeus, Jupiter. The High God and the Elements." *Zeitschrift für die alttestamentliche Wissenschaft* 106 (1994): 175–97.

———. *Israel and Hellas*. Berlin: de Gruyter, 1995.

Brown, Peter. *The Body and Society*. New York: Columbia Univ. Press, 1988.

Brownmiller, Susan. *Femininity*. New York: Simon and Schuster, 1984.

Bulkley, L. Duncan. *The Influence of the Menstrual Function on Certain Diseases of the Skin*. New York: Rebman Co, 1906.

Burkert, Walter. *Homo Necans*, translated by Peter Bing. Berkeley: Univ. of California Press, 1983.

———. *The Orientalizing Revolution*, translated by Margaret E. Pinder and W. Burkert. Cambridge, MA: Harvard Univ. Press, 1992.

Burnett, Anne. "Desire and Memory (Sappho Frag. 94)." *Classical Philology* 74 (1979): 6–27.

Burstein, Stanley M. *The Babylonica of Berossus*, vol. 1, fascicle 5. Malibu: Undena Publications, 1978.

Burton, Richard F., edited and translated by *The Book of the Thousand Nights and a Night*. 10 vols, 1886.

Cansdale, George. *All the Animals of the Bible Lands*. Grand Rapids: Zondervan, 1970.

Carmichael, Calum M. "'Treading' in the Book of Ruth." *Zeitschrift für die alttestamentliche Wissenschaft* 92 (1980): 248–66.

Carr, David M. "What Is Required to Identify Pre-Priestly Narrative Connections Between Genesis and Exodus? Some General Reflections and Specific Cases." In *A Farewell to The Yahwist?* edited by Thomas B. Dozeman and Konrad Schmid. Atlanta: Society of Biblical Literature, 2006.

Carson, Anne. "Putting Her in Her Place: Woman, Dirt, and Desire." In *Before Sexuality*, edited by David Halperin, John Winkler, et al. Princeton: Princeton Univ. Press, 1990.

Cassuto, Umberto. *The Documentary Hypothesis and the Composition of the Pentateuch*, translated by Israel Abrahams. Jerusalem: Magnes Press, 1941 (Hebrew), 1961 (English).

———. *A Commentary on the Book of Genesis*, vol. 1, translated by Israel Abrahams. Jerusalem: Magnes Press, 1944 (Hebrew), 1961 (English).

Cawkwell, G.L. "Early Greek Tyranny and the People." *Classical Quarterly* 45 (1995): 73–86.

Charmé, Stuart Z. "Children's Gendered Responses to the Story of Adam and Eve." *Journal of Feminist Studies in Religion* 13 (1997): 27–45.

Claburn, W. Eugne. "The Fiscal Basis of Josiah's Reforms." *Journal of Biblical Literature* 92 (1973): 11–22.

Clines, D.J.A. "The Tree of Knowledge and the Law of Yahweh." *Vetus Testamentum* 24 (1974): 8–14.

Clottes, Jean. *The Cave Beneath the Sea: Paleolithic Images at Cosquer*, translated by Marilyn Garner. New York: Harry N. Abrams, 1996.

Cogan, Mordecai and H. Tadmor, translator and commentator. *II Kings*. Anchor Bible. New York: Doubleday, 1988.

Cohen, H. Hirsch. *The Drunkenness of Noah*. University, AL: Univ. of Alabama Press, 1974.

Cohoon, J. W. and H. L. Crosby, translators. *Dio Chrysostom*. Loeb Classical Library, vol. 3, 33rd Discourse. Cambridge, MA: Harvard Univ. Press, 1951.

Collins, Terrence.. "The Physiology of Tears in the Old Testament: Part I." *Catholic Biblical Quarterly* 33 (1971): 18–38.

Condit, Ira. *The Fig.* Waltham: Chronica Botanica Co, 1947.

Cook, Stanley A. *The Religion of* Ancient *Palestine in the Light of Archaeology.* London: Oxford Univ. Press, 1930.

Cooper, Alan. "Ps 24: 7–10: Mythology and Exegesis." *Journal of Biblical Literature* 102 (1983): 37–60.

Cousteau, Jacques-Yves and Philippe Diole. *Diving Companions—Sea Lion, Elephant Seal, Walrus.* Garden City: Doubleday, 1974.

Crenshaw, James L. *Old Testament Wisdom: An Introduction.* Louisville: Westminster John Knox Press, 1998.

Crooke, W. "Some Notes on Homeric Folk-Lore." *Folklore* 19 (1908): 52–77, 153–89.

Cross, Frank Moore. *Canaanite Myth and Hebrew Epic.* Cambridge, MA: Harvard Univ. Press, 1973.

Dahood, Mitchell. "Ugaritic Studies and the Bible." *Gregorianum* 43 (1962): 55–79.

———. "Ebla, Genesis and John." *The Christian Century* 98 (1981): 418–21.

———. "Philological Observations on Five Biblical Texts." *Biblica* 63 (1982): 390–4.

Daly, Mary. *Beyond God the Father: Toward a Philosophy of Women's Liberation.* Boston: Beacon Press, 1973.

Daniel, Jerry L. "Anti-Semiticism in the Hellenistic-Roman Period." *Journal of Biblical Literature* 98 (1979): 45–65.

Das, Rahul Peter. "Problematic Aspects of the Sexual Rituals of the Bauls of Bengal." *Journal of the American Oriental Society* 112 (1992): 388–432.

Daube, David. *Studies in Biblical Law.* Cambridge: Cambridge Univ. Press, 1947.

———. "Direct and Indirect Causation in Biblical Law." *VT* 11 (1961): 246–69.

———.*Civil Disobedience in Antiquity.* Edinburgh: Edinburgh Univ. Press, 1972.

———. "Overpopulation: 1300 Years Ago." In *Medical and Genetic Ethics*. Oxford: Oxford Centre for Postgraduate Hebrew Studies, 1976.

Davies, Philip R. *In Search of 'Ancient Israel.'* Sheffield: Sheffield Academic Press, 1992.

Davidson, Arnold I. *The Emergence of Sexuality*. Cambridge, MA: Harvard Univ. Press, 2001.

Dawson, Warren R. "Egypt's Place in Medical History." In *Science, Medicine and History*, edited by E.A. Underload. London: Oxford Univ. Press, 1953.

Day, John. "Asherah in the Hebrew Bible and Northwest Semitic Literature." *Journal of Biblical Literature* 105 (1986): 385–408.

———. "Ugarit and the Bible: Do They Presuppose the Same Canaanite Mythology and Religion?" In *Ugarit and the Bible*, edited by George J. Brooke, Adrian H. Curtis, et al. Munster: Ugarit -Verlag, 1994.

———. *Yahweh and the Gods and Goddesses of Canaan*. Sheffield: Sheffield Academic Press, 2000.

Delaney, Carol. "Seeds of Honor, Fields of Shame." In *Honor and Shame and the Unity of the Mediterranean*, edited by David Glimmer. Special Publication 22. Washington, DC: American Anthropological Association, 1987.

Detienne, Marcel and Jean-Pierre Vernant. *Cunning Intelligence in Greek Culture and Society*, translated by Janet Lloyd. Sussex: Harvester Press, 1978.

Dever, William G. "Asherah, Consort of Yahweh? New Evidence from Kuntillet Ajrud." *Bulletin of the American Schools of Oriental Research* 255 (1984): 21–37.

———.*Recent Archaeological Discoveries and Biblical Research*. Seattle: Univ. of Washington Press, 1990.

Dietrich, B. C. *Death, Fate and the Gods*. London: Athlone Press, 1965.

Dillery, John. "The First Egyptian Narrative History: Manetho and Greek Historiography. *Zeitschrift fur Papyrologie und Epigraphik* 127 (1999): 93–127.

———. *Clio's Other Sons: Berossus and Manetho*. Ann Arbor: Univ. of Michigan Press, 2015.

Diole, Philippe. *4,000 Years under the Sea*. New York: Julian Messner, 1954.

Dodds, E. R. The Greeks and the Irrational. Eighth printing, 1973. Berkeley: Univ. of California Press, 1951.

Doria, Charles and Harris Lenowitz, eds., *Origins: Creation Texts from the Ancient Mediterranean*. Garden City: Anchor/Doubleday, 1976.

Douglas, Mary. *Leviticus as Literature*. Oxford: Oxford Univ. Press, 1999.

Dover, K. J. *Greek Popular Morality in the Time of Plato and Aristotle*. Berkeley: Univ. of California Press, 1974.

———. *Greek Homosexuality*. Cambridge, MA: Harvard Univ. Press, 1978.

Driver, G.R. "'Another Little Drink'—Isaiah 28:1–22." In *Words and Meanings: Essays Presented to David Winton Thomas*, edited by Peter R. Ackroyd and Barnabas Lindars. Cambridge: Cambridge Univ. Press, 1968.

DuBois, Page *Sowing the Body: Psychoanalysis and Ancient Representations of Women*. Chicago: Univ. of Chicago Press, 1988.

Duerr, Hans Peter. *Dreamtime*, translated by Felicitus Goodman. Oxford: Blackwell, 1985.

Dunson, William A. "Sea Snakes and the Sea Level Canal Controversy." In *The Biology of Sea Snakes*, edited by William A. Dunson. Baltimore: University Book Press, 1975.

Economist. "The Embryo's Canary," 323 (April 4, 1992):104.

Efros, Israel; Judah Kaufman; et al. *English-Hebrew Dictionary*. Tel-Aviv: Dvir Publishing Co., 1947.

Eitan, Israel. *A Contribution to Biblical Lexicography*. New York: Columbia Univ. Press, 1924.

———. "Two Onomatological Studies." *Journal of the American Oriental Society* 49 (1929): 30–3.

———. "Biblical Studies." In *Hebrew Union College Annual* 14 (1939).

Ehrenzweig, Anton. *The Psychoanalysis of Artistic Vision and Hearing*. London: Sheldon Press, 1975.

Eichrodt, Walther. *Ezekiel*, translated by Coslett Quin. Philadelphia: Westminster Press, 1970.

Eilberg-Schwartz, Howard. *God's Phallus and Other Problems for Men and Monotheism*. Paperback Edition. Boston: Beacon Press, 1994.

Engnell, Ivan. "Knowledge and Life in the Creation Story." In *Wisdom in Israel and in the Ancient Near East*, edited by Martin Noth and D. Winton Thomas. Leiden: Brill, 1969.

Entralgo, P. Lain. *The Therapy of the Word in Classical Antiquity*. New Haven: Yale Univ. Press, 1970.

Epstein, Claire. "Before History—the Golan's Chalcolithic Heritage." *Biblical Archaeology Review* 21 (1995).

Epstein, I., translator. *Babylonian Talmud* 35 vols. London: Soncino Press, 1938.

Erikson, Erik H. "On the Nature of Psychohistorical Evidence." In *Explorations in Psychohistory—The Wellfleet Papers*, edited by Robert Jay Lifton and E. Olson. New York: Simon and Schuster, 1974.

Fay, Edwin W. "Etymology and Slang." *American Journal of Philology* 21 (1900): 197–9.

———. "An Erroneous Phonetic Sequence." In *Studies in Honor of Basil L. Gildersleeve*. Baltimore: Johns Hopkins Univ. Press, 1902.

———. "Dreams, the Swelling Moon, the Sun." *Classical Quarterly* 11 (1917): 212–17.

Feldman, Louis H. *Josephus's Interpretation of the Bible*. Berkeley: Univ. of California Press, 1998.

Fenichel, Otto. *The Collected Papers of Otto Fenichel: First Series*, edited by Hanna Fenichel and David Rapaport. New York: Norton, 1953.

Ferenczi, Sandor. *Contributions to Psychoanalysis*, translated by Ernest Jones. Boston: Richard G. Badger, 1916.

———. *Thalassa: A Theory of Genitality*, translated by Henry Banker. Reprint. New York: Norton, 1968.

Finkel, Joshua. "An Interpretation of an Ugaritic Viticultural Poem. In *The Joshua Starr Memorial Volume*, edited by Abraham G. Duker. Philadelphia: Maurice Jacobs Press, 1953.

Finkelstein, Israel. "A Low Chronology Update." In *The Bible and Radiocarbon Dating,* edited by Thomas E. Levy and Thomas Higham. London: Equinox Publishing, 2005.

Finkelstein, Israel and Neil Asher Silberman. *The Bible Unearthed.* New York: Free Press, 2001.

Finley, M.I. "The Elderly in Classical Antiquity." *Greece and Rome* 28 (1981): 156–71.

Fishbane, Michael. *Text and Texture.* New York: Schocken, 1979.

———. *The Garments of Torah: Essays in Biblical Hermeneutics.* Bloomington: Indiana Univ. Press, 1989.

Fleming, Carol B. "Maidens of the sea can be alluring, but sailor beware." *Smithsonian* 14 (1983): 86–95.

Fohrer, Georg. "Twofold Aspects of Hebrew Words." In *Words and Meanings,* edited by P.R. Ackroyd and B. Lindars. Cambridge: Cambridge Univ. Press, 1968.

Fokkelman, J.P., "Genesis." In *The Literary Guide to the Bible,* edited by Robert Alter and Frank Kermode. Cambridge, MA: Harvard Univ. Press, 1987.

Fontenrose, Joseph. "Dagon and El." *Oriens* 10 (1957): 277–9.

———. "White Goddess and Syrian Goddess." *University of California Publications in Semitic Philology,* edited by Walter Fischel. 11 (1951): 125–48.

Forbes, Robert J. *Studies in Ancient Technology.* Vol. 3. Leiden: Brill, 1965.

Fowler, Brenda. "Recreating Stone Tools to Learn Makers' Ways. *New York Times* (New York), December 20, 1994.

Fowler, M. "Castle Kennedy Fig." *Journal of Horticulture and Cottage Gardening* n.s. 8 (1865).

Freedman, H. and M. Simon. *Midrash Rabbah.* 10 vols. London: Soncino Press, 1939.

Freeman, Charles. *Egypt, Greece and Rome: Civilizations of the Ancient Mediterranean.* New York: Oxford Univ. Press, 1996.

Freeman, Derek. "Severed Heads That Germinate." In *Fantasy and Symbol,* edited by R. H. Hook. London: Academic Press, 1979.

Friedl, Ernestine. "Sex the Invisible." *American Anthropologist* 96 (1994): 833–41.

Friedman, Richard Elliott. *Who Wrote the Bible?* New York: Summit/Simon and Schuster, 1987.

Frye, Northrop. *Words with Power: Being a Second study of "The Bible and Literature"* San Diego: Harcourt, 1990.

Galen. *On Anatomical Procedures,* translated by W. H. L. Duckworth. Cambridge: Cambridge Univ. Press, 1962.

———. *On the Usefulness of the Parts of the Body,* translated by M. T. May. Ithaca: Cornell Univ. Press, 1968.

Galil, J. "An Ancient Technique for Ripening Sycamore Fruit in East Mediterranean Countries." *Economic Botany* 22 (1968): 178–90.

Gaster, T.H. "Folklore Motifs in Canaanite Myth." *Journal of the Royal Asiatic Society* 71 (1944): 30–51.

Geddes, Arthur. "Creation, and the Blessing or the Curse upon Fruitfulness: An Anthropological Interpretation of Genesis I–III." *Man* 45, no. 104 (1945): 123–8.

Gellius. *The Attic Nights of Aulus Gellius,* translated by John C. Rolfe. Loeb Classical Library. Reprint of 1927 edition. Cambridge, MA: Harvard Univ. Press, 1952.

Giacomelli, Anne. "Aphrodite and After." *Phoenix* 34 (1980): 1–19.

Gimbutas, Marija. *The Language of the Goddess.* New York: Harper and Row, 1989.

Glueck, Nelson. *Rivers in the Desert: A History of the Negev.* New York: Grove Press, 1960.

Golden, Mark. "Did the Ancients Care When Their Children Died?" *Greece and Rome* 35 (1988): 152–163.

Goldziher, Ignaz. *Mythology Among the Hebrews and Its Historical Development.* Reprint of 1877 edition. New York: Cooper Square Publisher, 1967.

Goleman, Daniel. "Failing to Recognize Bias in Science." *Technology Review* 90 (1987): 26–7.

Goodenough, Erwin R. *Jewish Symbols in the Greco-Roman Period*. Vols. 5, 6, 8. New York: Pantheon, 1956.

Goodrich Freer, Adela. *Arabs in Tent and Town*. London: Seeley, Service and Co., 1924.

Gopnik, Alison. *The Philosophical Baby: What Children's Minds Tell Us about Truth, Love, and the Meaning of Life*. New York: Farrar, Straus, 2009.

Gordis, Robert. "The Significance of the Paradise Myth." *American Journal of Semitic Languages* 52–3 (1935–37): 86–94.

———. "Studies in Hebrew Roots of Contrasted Meanings." *Jewish Quarterly Review* 27 (1936): 33–58.

———. "Studies in the Relationship of Biblical and Rabbinic Hebrew." In *Louis Ginzberg Jubilee Volume*. New York: American Academy for Jewish Research, 1945.

———. "Commentary on the Text of Lamentations." In *The Seventy-Fifth Anniversary Volume of the Jewish Quarterly Review*, edited by Abraham A. Neuman and Solomon Zeitlin. Philadelphia: Jewish Quarterly Review, 1967.

———. "On Methodology in Biblical Exegesis." *Jewish Quarterly Review* 60 (1970): 93–118.

———. *The Book of Job: Commentary*. New York: Jewish Theological Seminary, 1978.

Gordon, Cyrus H. *The World of the Old Testament*. Garden City: Doubleday, 1958.

———. *The Common Background of Greek and Hebrew Civilizations*. New York: Norton, 1965.

———. "Review of Books." *Journal of the American Oriental Society* 100 (1980): 354–7.

———. "Asymmetric Janus Parallelism." *Eretz-Israel*. Jerusalem: Israel Exploration Society, 1982.

———. "Ebla as Background for the Old Testament." In *Supplements to Vetus Testamentum*. Vol. 40. Leiden: Brill, 1988.

———. "'This Time' (Genesis 2:23)." In *Sha'arei Talmon: Studies in the Bible, Qumran and the Ancient Near East Presented to Shemaryahu Talmon*, ed. Michael Fishbane, Emanuel Tov et al. Winona Lake: Eisenbrauns, 1992.

Gottwald, Norman K. *The Hebrew Bible: A Socio-Literary Introduction*. Philadelphia: Fortress Press, 1987.

———. "From Tribal Existence to Empire: The Socio-Historical Context for the Rise of the Hebrew Prophets." In *God and Creation*, edited by J. M. Thomas and V. Visick. Madison: A-R Editions, 1991.

Graf, Fritz. *Magic in the Ancient World*, translated by Franklin Philip. Cambridge, MA: Harvard Univ. Press, 1997.

Granger, Herbert. "Deformed Kinds and the Fixity of Species." *Classical Quarterly* 37 (1987): 110–16.

Gray, George Buchanan. *Numbers*. International Critical Commentary. New York: Charles Scribner's Sons, 1906.

Gray, John. *I & II Kings*. Philadelphia: Westminster, 1970.

Grayson, A. K. "Assyrian Civilization." In *The Cambridge Ancient History*. Vol 3. Second edition. Cambridge: Cambridge Univ. Press 1993.

Greek Vases from the Hirschmann Collection, edited by H. Bloesch. Zurich: Verlag Hans Rohr, 1982.

Greenblatt, Stephen. *The Rise and Fall of Adam and Eve*. New York: Norton, 2017.

Greene, Mott T. *Natural Knowledge in Preclassical Antiquity*. Baltimore: Johns Hopkins Univ. Press, 1992.

Greenberg, Moshe. *Ezekiel 1–20*. Anchor Bible, vol. 22. Garden City: Doubleday, 1983.

Greenfield, Jonas C. "Lexicographical Notes I." *Hebrew Union College Annual*. 29 (1958): 203–28.

———. "The Seven Pillars of Wisdom (Prov. 9:1) —A Mistranslation." *Jewish Quarterly Review* 76 (1985): 13–20.

———. "Apkallu." In *Dictionary of Deities and Demons in the Bible*, edited by Karel van der Toorn et al. Leiden: Brill, 1995.

Greenfield, Jonas C. and Aaron Shaffer. "Notes on the Akkadian-Aramaic Bilingual Statue from Tell Fekherye." *Iraq* 45 (1983): 109–16.

Griffin, Jasper. *Homer on Life and Death*. New York: Oxford Univ. Press, 1980.

Grof, Stanislav. *Realms of Human Unconscious*. New York: Viking, 1975.

Guillaume, Alfred. *Hebrew and Arabic Lexicography*. Leiden: Brill, 1965.

Gulik, Robert H. van. *Sexual Life in Ancient China*. Leiden: Brill, 1961.

Hadley, Judith M. *The Cult of Asherah in Ancient Israel and Judah: Evidence for a Hebrew Goddess*. Cambridge: Cambridge Univ. Press, 2000.

Hallo, William W. "Texts, Statues and the Cult of the Divine King." In *Congress Volume Jerusalem 1986*, edited by J. A. Emerton. Leiden: Brill, 1988.

Halperin, David J. *Seeking Ezekiel*. State College: Penn State Univ. Press, 1993.

Halpern, Baruch. "Brisker Pipes Than Poetry: The Development of Israelite Monotheism." In *Judaic Perspectives on Ancient Israel*, edited by Jacob Neusner, Baruch Levine, et al. Philadelphia: Fortress Press, 1987.

Hamblin. Dora Jane. "Has the Garden of Eden Been Located at Last?" *Smithsonian* 18 (1987): 127–35.

Haran, M. "Literacy and Schools in Ancient Israel." In *Congress Volume Jerusalem 1986*, edited by J. A. Emerton. Leiden: Brill, 1988.

Harper, William R. *Introductory Hebrew Method and Manual*. 1885. Revised by J.M. Powis Smith. Chicago: Univ. of Chicago Press, 1959.

Harrison, Peter *The Bible, Protestantism, and the Rise of Natural Science*. Cambridge: Cambridge Univ. Press, 1998.

Hasel, Gerhard F. and Michael G. Hasel. "The Hebrew Term *'ed* in Gen 2,6 and Its Connection in Ancient Near Eastern Literature." *Zeitschrift für die alttestamentliche Wissenschaft* 112 (2000): 321–40.

Haupt, Paul. "To know = to have sexual commerce." *Journal of Biblical Literature* 34 (1915): 71–5.

———. "Assyrian *lanu*, 'aspect'—Arabic *laun*, 'color.'" *Journal of the American Oriental Society* 37 (1917): 235–55.

———. "Brief Communications—Pelican and Bittern." *Journal of Biblical Literature* 39 (1920a): 158–61.

———. "Heb. *mardut,* chastisement and chastity." *Journal of Biblical Literature* 39 (1920b): 156–8.

———. "Heb. *ra,* evil = Arab. *'urr.*" *Journal of Biblical Literature* 39 (1920c): 152–5.

———. "*Qas,* straw, and *qast,* bow." *Journal of Biblical Literature* 39 (1920d): 161–3.

———. "Philological and Archeological Studies." *American Journal of Philology* 45 (1924): 238–59.

———. "Etymological and Critical Notes." *American Journal of Philology* 47 (1926): 305–18.

Hayman, Peter. "Monotheism—A Misused Word In Jewish Studies?" *Journal of Jewish Studies* 42 (1991): 1–15.

Healey, J. F. "The Underworld Character of the God Dagan." *Journal of Northwest Semitic Languages* 5 (1977): 43–51.

Heidel, Alexander. *The Gilgamesh Epic and the Old Testament Parallels.* 2nd ed. Chicago: Univ. of Chicago Press, 1949.

———. *The Babylonian Genesis.* Phoenix, edited by Chicago: Univ. of Chicago Press, 1963.

Hendel, Ronald S. "Of Demigods and the Deluge: Toward an Interpretation of Genesis 6:1–4." *Journal of Biblical Literature* 106 (1987): 13–26.

Henderson, Jeffrey. *The Maculate Muse.* New Haven: Yale Univ. Press, 1975.

Herodotus. *The History,* translated by David Greene. Chicago: Univ. of Chicago Press, 1987.

Herrmann, Siegfried. "Observations on Some Recent Hypotheses Pertaining to Early Israelite History." In *Justice and Righteousness,* edited by Henning Graf Reventlow and Yair Hoffman. Sheffield: Journal for the Study of the Old Testament Press, 1992.

Herzog, Chaim and Mordechai Gichon. *Battles of the Bible.* London: Greenhill Books, 1997.

Hesiod. *The Homeric Hymns and Homerica.* Reprinted 1982, translated by H. G. Evelyn-White. London: Heinemann, 1914.

———. *The Theogany,* translation and commentary by M. L. West. Oxford: Clarendon Press, 1966.

———. *Works and Days,* translation and commentary by M. L. West. Oxford: Clarendon Press, 1978.

Hess, Eckhard H. "Attitude and Pupil Size." *Scientific American* 212, no. 4 (1965): 46–54.

Hess, Richard S. "Hezekiah and Sennacherib in 2 Kings 18–20." In *Zion, City of Our God,* edited by Richard S. Hess and Gordon J. Wenham. Grand Rapids: Eerdmans, 1999.

Hibbitts, Bernard J. "'Coming to Our Senses': Communication and Legal Expression in Performance Cultures." *Emory Law Journal* 41 (1992): 874–960.

Hiebert, Theodore. *The Yahwist's Landscape: Nature and Religion in Early Israel.* New York: Oxford Univ. Press, 1996. Paperback edition. Minneapolis: Fortress Press, 2008.

Hillel, Daniel. *The Natural History of the Bible: An Environmental Exploration of the Hebrew Scriptures.* New York: Columbia Univ. Press, 2006.

Hillers, D. R. "Dust: Some Aspects of Old Testament Imagery." In *Love and Death in the Ancient Near East: Essays in Honor of Marvin Pope,* edited by J. H. Marks and R. M. Good. Guilford, CT: Four Quarters, 1987.

Hillman, James. *The Myth of Analysis: Three Essays in Archetypal Psychology.* Evanston: Northwestern Univ. Press, 1972.

Hoffman, Dustin. *Sun-Sentinel* (Fort Lauderdale, Florida), January 1, 1979.

Hoffmeier, James K. *Israel in Egypt.* New York: Oxford Univ. Press, 1997.

Hoffner, Harry A., Jr. "Incest, Sodomy and Bestiality in the Ancient Near East." In *Orient and Occident: Essays Presented to Cyrus H. Gordon on the Occasion of His Sixty-fifth Birthday,* edited by Harry A. Hoffner, Jr. Altes Orient und Altes Testament. Vol. 22 (1973). Neukirchen-Vluya: Neukirchener Verlag, 81–90.

Homer. *The Iliad,* translated by A.T. Murray. Loeb Classical Library. London: William Heinemann, 1937.

———. *The Odyssey,* translated by by Richard Lattimore. New York: Harper and Row, 1967.

Horowitz, Helen L. *Rereading Sex*. New York: Knopf, 2002.

Hrdlicka, Ales. "Quadruped Progression in the Human Child." *American Journal of Physical Anthropology* 10 (1927): 347–54.

Interpreter's Bible, The. Vol. 1. New York: Abingdon Cokesbury Press, 1952.

Isler, Hans Peter. *Greek Vases from the Hirschmann Collection,* edited by Hansjorg Bloesch. Zurich: Verlag Hans Rohr, 1982.

Iwry, S. "New Evidence for Belomancy in Ancient Palestine and Phoenicia." *Journal of the American Oriental Society* 81 (1961): 27–34.

Jacobs, Noah J. *Naming-Day in Eden*. New York: Macmillan, 1958.

Jacobsen, Thorkild. "Toward the Image of Tammuz.: *History of Religion* 1 (1961): 189–213.

———. *The Treasures of Darkness*. New Haven: Yale Univ. Press, 1976.

Jamieson-Drake, David W. *Scribes and Scholars in Monarchic Judah*. Sheffield: Journal of the Study of the Old Testament Press, 1991.

Jarvis, C. S. *Yesterday and Today in Sinai*. Boston: Houghton Mifflin, 1932.

Jastrow, Marcus. *A Dictionary of the Targumim, the Talmud Babli and Yerushalmi, and the Midrashic Literature*. 2 vols. 1903 Reprint. New York: Pardes Publishing, 1950.

Jerusalem Bible. Garden City: Doubleday, 1966.

Johns, Catherine. *Sex or Symbol*. Austin: Univ. of Texas Press, 1982.

Joines, Karen Randolph. "Winged Serpents in Isaiah's Inaugural Vision." *Journal of Biblical Literature* 86 (1967): 10–15.

———. "The Bronze Serpent in the Israelite Cult." *Journal of Biblical Literature* 87 (1968): 245–56.

Jones, Bryan. "Irish Folklore from Cavan, Meath, Kerry, and Limerick." *Folklore* 19 (1908): 315–23.

Jones, Ernest. *Papers on Psycho-Analysis*. 4th edition. Baltimore: William Wood & Co., 1938.

———. *Essays in Applied Psycho-Analysis*. Vol. 2. London: Hogarth Press, 1951.

Joyce, James. *A Portrait of the Artist*. 13th printing. New York: Viking, 1969.

Kahler, Erich, *The Disintegration of Form in the Arts*. New York: George Braziller, 1968.

Kandel, Eric R. *In Search of Memory*. New York: Norton, 2006.

Karmon, Yehuda. *Israel*. London: Wiley-Interscience, 1971.

Kautzsch, E., editor. *Gesenius' Hebrew Grammar*, translated by A.E. Cowley. 2nd edition. 1910. Reprint. Oxford: Clarendon Press, 1949.

Von Kellenbach, Katharina. *Anti-Judaism in Feminist Religious Writings*. Atlanta: Scholars Press, 1994.

Kerenyi, C. *The Gods of the Greeks*, Translated by Norman Cameron. Reprint. London: Thames and Hudson, 1979.

Kermode, Frank. "In the Beginning." Review of *A Literary Bible: An Original Translation*, by David Rosenberg. *New York Times Book Review*, January 3, 2010.

Keuls, Eva C. *The Reign of the Phallus*. Berkeley: Univ. of California Press, 1993.

Kilmer, Anne Draffkorn. "The Mesopotamian Counterparts of the Biblical Nephilim." In *Perspectives on Language and Text*, edited by Edgar W. Conrad and Edward G. Newing. Winona Lake: Eisenbrauns, 1987.

King, Judith E. "The Monk Seals (Genus Monachus)." In *British Museum (Natural History) Bulletin, Zoology*. Vol. 3, no. 5. (1956).

King, Philip J. "The Eighth, the Greatest of Centuries?" *Journal of biblical Literature* 108 (1989): 3–15.

Kinsey, Alfred C., Wardell B. Pomeroy, et al. *Sexual Behavior in the Human Female*. Philadelphia: W. B. Saunders, 1953.

Kitchen, K.A. *Ancient Orient and Old Testament*. Chicago: Inter-varsity Press, 1968.

———. *The Bible in Its World: The Bible and Archeology Today*. Chicago: Inter-varsity Press, 1977.

Kluver, Heinrich. *Mescal and Mechanisms of Hallucinations*. Chicago: Univ. of Chicago Press, 1966.

Knight, Chris. *Blood Relations*. New Haven: Yale Univ. Press, 1991.

Kolakowski, Leszek. *Religion*. New York: Oxford Univ. Press, 1982.

Kooij, Arie van der. "The Septuagint of the Pentateuch and Ptolemaic Rule." In *The Pentateuch as Torah: New Models for Understanding Its Promulgation and Acceptance,* edited by Gary N. Knoppers and Bernard M. Levinson. Winona Lake: Eisenbrauns, 2007.

Kraemer, Ross Shepard. *Her Share of the Blessings.* New York: Oxford Univ. Press, 1992.

Kramer, Samuel Noah and John Maier. *Myths of Enki, the Crafty God.* New York: Oxford Univ. Press, 1989.

Kugel, James L. *The Bible as It Was.* Cambridge, MA: Harvard Univ. Press, 1999.

Kugler, Paul. *The Alchemy of Discourse.* Lewisburg: Bucknell Univ. Press, 1982.

Kutscher, E.Y. *A History of the Hebrew Language,* edited by Raphael Kutscher. Jerusalem: Magnes Press, 1982.

Kugelmann, Robert. *The Windows of Soul.* Lewisburg: Bucknell Univ. Press, 1983.

Labuschagne, C.J. "The Crux in Ruth 4:11." *Zeitschrift für die alttestamentliche Wissenschaft* 79 (1967): 364–67.

Lambert, W.G. "Old Testament Mythology in Its Ancient Near Eastern Context." In *Congress Volume Jerusalem 1986,* edited by J.A. Emerton. Leiden: Brill, 1988.

Landy, Francis. *Paradoxes of Paradise: Identity and Difference in the Song of Songs.* Sheffield: Almond Press, 1983.

———. "Seraphim and Poetic Process." In *The Labour of Reading: desire, alienation, and biblical interpretation,* edited by Fiona C. Black, Roland Boer, et al. Atlanta: Society of Biblical Literature, 1999.

Lawrence, D.H. *Collected Poems of D. H. Lawrence.* London: William Heinemann, 1933.

Laws, R.M. *The Elephant Seal II. General, Social and Reproductive Behavior.* Falkland Islands Dependencies Survey, Scientific Reports, no. 13. London: By Her Majesty's Stationery Office, 1956.

Layton, Scott C. "Remarks on the Canaanite Origin of Eve." *Catholic Biblical Quarterly* 59 (1997): 22–32.

Leupold, H. C. "Genesis." In *The Biblical Expositor,* edited by C. F. H. Henry. Philadelpha: A.J. Holman, 1973.

Lévi-Strauss, Claude. *Tristes Tropiques,* translated by John and Doreen Weightman. New York: Atheneum.

Lévi-Strauss and Didier Eribon. *Conversations with Claude Lévi-Strauss,* translated by Paula Wissing. Chicago: Univ. of Chicago Press, 1991.

Levin, Saul. *The Father of Joshua/Jesus.* Binghamton: State Univ. of New York, 1978.

Levinson, Bernard M. "The Right Chorale: From the Poetics to the Hermeneutics of the Hebrew Bible." In *Not in Heaven: Coherence and Complexity in Biblical Narrative,* edited by Jason P. Rosenblatt and Joseph C. Sitterson, Jr. Bloomington: Indiana Univ. Press, 1991.

———. *Deuteronomy and the Hermeneutics of Legal Innovation.* New York: Oxford Univ. Press, 1997.

Levison, John R. "The Exoneration of Eve in the Apocalypse of Moses 15–30." *Journal for the Study of Judaism* 20 (1989): 135–50.

Lewis, Charlton T. and Charles Short. *A Latin Dictionary.* 1st ed., 1879. Oxford: Clarendon Press, 1962.

Lewis, I. M. *Ecstatic Religion.* Baltimore: Penguin Books, 1971.

Lewis, Theodore J. *Cults of the Dead in Ancient Israel and Ugarit.* Altanta: Scholars Press, 1989.

Liddel, Henry G., Robert Scott, and Henry S. Jones. *A Greek-English Lexicon.* 1st ed.,1843. Oxford: Clarendon Press, 1961.

Lilja, Saara. "The Treatment of Odours in the Poetry of Antiquity." *Commentationes Humanarum Litterarum.* Vol. 49. Helsinki: Societas Scientiarum Fennica, 1972.

Lissarraguje, Francois. "The Sexual Life of Satyrs." In *Before Sexuality,* edited by David M. Halperin et al. Princeton: Princeton Univ Press, 1990.

Ljung, Inger. *Silence or Suppression: Attitudes Towards Women in the Old Testament.* Uppsala: S. Academiae Ubsaliensis, 1989.

Loader, J.A. "The Concept of Darkness in the Hebrew Root RB/RP." In *De Fructu Oris Sui*. Pretoria Oriental Series, edited by J.H. Eybers, F.C. Fensham, et al. Vol. 9. Leiden: Brill, 1971.

Lockley, Ronald M. *The Seals and The Curragh*. London: J. M. Dent and Sons, 1954.

———. *Grey Seal, Common Seal: An Account of the Life Histories of British Seals.* New York: October House, 1966.

Lorenz, Konrad. *Civilized Man's Eight Deadly Sins,* translated by Marjorie Kerr Wilson. New York: Harcourt Brace, 1974.

———. *The Waning of Humaneness,* Translated by R.W. Kickert. Boston: Little Brown, 1987.

Lorimer, H.L. "Dipaltos." [in Greek] *The Annual of the British School at Athens.* Vol. 37. London: Macmillan, 1940.

Lucian of Samosata. *The Syrian Goddess (De Dea Syria),* translated by Harold W. Attridge and Robert A. Oden. Missoula: Scholars Press, 1976.

Lucretius. *De Rerum Natura,* translated by W.H.D. Rouse. Loeb Classical Library. Cambridge, MA: Harvard Univ. Press, 1943.

Lutz, H. F. "The hagoroth of Genesis 3:7." *Journal of the American Oriental Society* 42 (1922): 208–9.

Lutzky, Harriet. "Short Notes." *Vetus Testamentum* 46 (1996) :?–124.

———. "Shadday as a Goddess Epithet." *Vetus Testamentum* 48 (1998): 15–36.

McCartney, Eugene S. "Sex Determination and Sex Control in Antiquity." *American Journal of Philology* 43 (1922): 62–70.

McEvenue, Sean E. "The Political Structure in Judah from Cyrus to Nehemiah." *Catholic Biblical Quarterly* 44 (1981): 353–64.

Machinist, Peter. "Literature as Politics: The Tukulti-Ninurta Epic and the Bible." *Catholic Biblical Quarterly* 38 (1976): 455–82.

Macht, David I. "A Scientific Appreciation of Leviticus 12: 1–5." *Journal of Biblical Literature* 52 (1933): 253–60.

Macht, David I. and William M. Kunkel. "Concerning the Antispectic Action of Some Aromatic Fumes." In *Proceedings of the Society for Experimental Biology and Medicine* 18 (1920–21): 68–70.

Macht, David I. and Dorothy S. Lubin.. "A Phyto-Pharmacological Study of Menstrual Toxin." *Journal of Pharmacology and Experimental Therapy* 22 (1923): 413–66.

McKay, J.W. *Religion in Judah under the Assyrians*. London: SCM Press, 1973.

Mackie, George. *Bible Manners and Customs*. New York: Fleming H. Revell Co.

143–53, n.d.

Maier, Walter A., III. *Asherah: Extrabiblical Evidence*. Atlanta: Scholars Press, 1986.

Majno, Guido. *The Healing Hand: Man and Wound in the Ancient World*. Cambridge, MA: Harvard Univ. Press, 1975.

Makarius, Laura. "Children of Impurity." *Diogenes* 112 (1980): 26–51.

Mallowan, M.E.L. *Nimrud and Its Remains*. 3 vols. New York: Dodd, Mead, 1966.

Manger, Itzig. "Abishag Writes A Letter Home." In *An Anthology of Modern Yiddish Poetry*, edited by R. Whitman. New York: October House, 1966.

Manniche, Lisa. *Sexual Life in Ancient Egypt*. London: KPI Ltd., 1987.

Mansfield, J. "Heraclitus on the Psychology and Physiology of Sleep and on Rivers." *Mnemosyne*, series 4, 20 (1967): 1–29.

Marcos, Natalio Fernandez. *The Septuagint in Context*, Translated by Wilfred G.E. Watson. Leiden: Brill, 2000.

Margalit, Baruch. "Some Observations on the Inscription and Drawing from Khirbet el-Qom." *Vetus Testamentum* 39 (1989a): 371–8.

———. *The Ugaritic Poem of AQHT*. Berlin: Walter de Gruyter, 1989b.

———. "The Meaning and Significance of Asherah." *Vetus Testamentum* 40 (1990): 264–97.

Margalith, Othniel. "A New Type of Asherah-Figurine?" *Vetus Testamentum* 44 (1994): 109–15.

Marinatos, Nanno. *Minoan Religion: Ritual, Image, and Symbol*. Columbia, SC: Univ. of South Carolina Press, 1993.

Martin, Richard Mark. *Mammals of the Ocean*. New York: Putnam, 1977.

Mason, Wyatt "Homer's Daughter." *The New York Times Magazine*, November 2017.

Mattern, Vicki. "Discover Figs for Your World!" *Organic Gardening* 38 (1991): 30–5.

Maxwell, Gavin. *Seals of the World.* Boston: Houghton Mifflin, 1957.

Mayes, Andrew D.H. "Deuteronomic Ideology and the Theology of the Old Testament." *Journal for the Study of the Old Testament* 82:57–81.

Mayor, Adrienne. *The First Fossil Hunters: Paleontology in Greek and Roman Times*. Princeton: Princeton Univ. Press, 2000.

McKenzie, D. *Aromatics and the Soul*. New York: Paul B. Hoeber, 1923.

Mendenhall, George E. "The Worship of Baal and Asherah." In *Biblical and Related Studies Presented to Samuel Iwry*, edited by A. Kort and S. Morschauser. Winona Lake: Eisenbrauns, 1985.

Meyers, Carol. "Roots of Restriction: Women in Early Israel." In *The Bible and Liberation*, edited by Norman Gottwald. Maryknoll: Orbis, 1984.

———. "Gender Roles and Genesis 3:16 Revisited." In *A Feminist Companion to Genesis*, edited by A. Brenner. Sheffield: Sheffield Academic Press, 1993.

———. *Households and Holiness*. Minneapolis: Fortress Press, 2005.

———. *Rediscovering Eve: Ancient Israelite Women in Context*. Oxford: Oxford Univ. Press, 2013.

Meyers, Eric M. "The Persian Period of the Judean Restoration: From Zerubbabel to Nehemiah." In *Ancient Israelite Religion*, edited by Patrick D. Miller, Jr., Paul D. Hanson, et al. Philadelphia: Fortress, 1987.

Mikalson, Jon D. *Religion in Hellenistic Athens*. Berkeley: Univ. of California Press, 1998.

Miles, Margaret R. *Carnal Knowing*. Boston: Beacon Press, 1989.

Milgrom, Jacob. *The JPS Torah Commentary: Numbers*. Philadelphia: Jewish Publication Society, 1990.

Miller, Arthur. *The Creation of the World and Other Business*. New York: Viking, 1972.

———. "The Story of Adam and Eve." In *Genesis as it is Written: Contemporary Writers on Our First Stories,* edited by David Rosenberg. San Francisco: HarperCollins, 1996.

Miller, Patrick D., Jr. *The Divine Warrior*. Cambridge, MA: Harvard Univ. Press, 1973.

———. "Aspects of the Religion of Ugarit." In *Ancient Israelite Religion,* edited by Patrick D. Miller Jr., Paul Hanson, et al. Philadelphia: Fortress, 1987.

Miller, Patrick D., Jr. and J. J. M. Roberts. *The Hand of the Lord*. Baltimore: Johns Hopkins Univ. Press, 1977.

Mitchell, T. C. "The Fall of Samaria." In *The Cambridge Ancient History*. Vol. 3. Cambridge: Cambridge Univ. Press, 1993.

Mittelbach, Margaret and M. Crewdson. "Wild Life: Return of the Seals to Long Island." *New York Times,* March 26, 1999.

Moberly, R.W.L. "Did the Serpent Get it Right?" *Journal of Theological Studies,* n.s., 39 (1988): 1–27.

Momigliano, Arnaldo. *Alien Wisdom*. Cambridge: Cambridge Univ. Press, 1975.

Montgomery, James A. "Some Hebrew Etymologies." *Jewish Quarterly Review* 25 (1935): 261–269.

Moor, Johannes C. de. "East of Eden." *Zeitschrift für die alttestamentliche Wissenschaft* 100 (1988): 105–11.

Morgenstern, Julian. "Jerusalem—485 B.C." *Hebrew Union College Annual* 27 (1956): 101–79.

Morris, Desmond. *The Naked Ape*. New York: McGraw-Hill, 1967.

Mowinckel, Sigmund. "Shhl." [in Hebrew] In *Hebrew and Semitic Studies Presented to G. R. Driver,* edited by D. W. Thomas and W. D. McHardy. Oxford: Clarendon Press, 1963.

Mullen, E. Theodore, Jr. *The Assembly of the Gods*. Chico: Scholars Press, 1980.

Mundkur, Balaji. *The Cult of the Serpent*. Albany: State Univ. of New York Press, 1983.

Murray, Gilbert *Five Stages of Greek Religion*. Garden City: Doubleday Anchor, 1955.

Myers, Jacob M., translator and commentator. *Ezra. Nehemiah,* Garden City: Doubleday, 1965.

Naccache, Albert F.H. "El's Abode in his Land." In *Ugarit, Religion and Culture,* edited by N. Wyatt, W. G. E. Watson, et al. Munster: Ugarit-Verlag, 1996.

Nachmanides. *Commentary on the Torah*. Vols. 3 and 5, translated by Charles B. Chavel. New York: Shilo, 1974.

Nagy, Gregory. *Comparative Studies in Greek and Indic Meter*. Cambridge, MA: Harvard Univ. Press, 1974.

———. *Greek Mythology and Poetics*. Ithaca: Cornell Univ. Press, 1990.

Nakanose, Shigeyuki. *Josiah's Passover: Sociology and the Liberating Bible*. Maryknoll: Orbis, 1993.

Neumann, Erich. *The Origins and History of Consciousness,* translated by R. F. C. Hull. New York: Harper Torchbooks, 1962.

Neusner, Jacob. *Genesis Rabbah—A New American Translation,* translated and annotated by Jacob Neusner. Vol. 1. Atlanta: Scholars Press, 1985.

———. *Confronting Creation*. Columbia: Univ. of South Caroline Press, 1991.

Neusner, Jacob and William Scott Green, editors. *The Dictionary of Judaism in the Biblical Period*. New York: Macmillan, 1996.

Nicholson, Ernest W. *God and His People*. Oxford: Clarendon Press, 1986.

Nickelsburg, George W.E., translator and commentator *1 Enoch*. Minneapolis: Fortress, 2001.

Nicol, George G. "The Chronology of Genesis: Genesis XXVI 1–33 as 'Flashback.'" *Vetus Testamentum* 46 (1996), 3.

Niditch, Susan. *Oral Word and Written Word: Ancient Israelite Literature*. Louisville: Westminster, 1996.

Nohrnberg, James C. "The Keeping of Nahor." In *The Book and the Text,* edited by Regina M. Schwartz. Oxford: Blackwell, 1990.

Noth, Martin and D. Winton Thomas, eds. *Wisdom in Israel and in the Ancient Near East. Supplements to Vetus Testamentum, III*. Leiden: Brill, 1969.

Oe, Kenzaburo. *A Personal Matter,* translated by John Nathan. New York: Grove Press, 1968.

O'Faolain, Julia and Lauro Marmes. *Not in God's Image.* New York: Harper Colophon, 1973.

O'Flaherty, Wendy Doniger. "The Submarine Mare in the Mythology of Shiva." *Journal Royal Asiatic Society* (1971): 9–27.

———. *Women, Androgynes, and Other Mythical Beasts.* Chicago: Univ. of Chicago Press, 1980.

Oldenburg, Ulf. *The Conflict Between El and Baal in Canaanite Religion.* Leiden: Brill, 1969.

Oldfather, L. H., translator. *Diodorus of Sicily,* Loeb Classical Library. London: William Heinemann, 1939.

Olyan, Saul M. *Asherah and the Cult of Yahweh in Israel.* Atlanta: Scholars Press, 1988.

Onians, Richard Broxton. *The Origins of European Thought: About the Body, the Mind, the Soul, the World, Time, and Fate.* 2nd ed. Cambridge: Cambridge Univ. Press, 1954.

Oppenheim, A. Leo. *Ancient Mesopotamia.* Chicago: Univ. of Chicago Press, 1964.

Oppian. *Halieutica,* translated by A. W. Mair. Loeb Classical Library. London: William Heinemann, 1928.

Orel, Vladimir. "The Great Fall of Dagon." *Zeitschrift für die Alttestamentliche Wissenschaft* 110 (1998): 427–32.

Orlinsky, Harry. "Septuagint as Holy Writ." *Hebrew Union College Annual* 46 (1975): 89–114.

———. "The Septuagint and Its Hebrew Text." In *The Cambridge History of Judaism,* Vol. 2, edited by W. D. Davies and Louis Finkelstein. Cambridge: Cambridge Univ. Press, 1984.

Orni, Efraim and Elisha Efrat. *Geography of Israel.* 3rd revised edition. Philadelphia: Jewish Publication Society, 1971.

Orwell, George. *A Collection of Essays.* New York: Doubleday Anchor Books, 1954.

Ottosson, M. "Eden and the Land of Promise." In *Congress Volume Jerusalem 1986*, edited by J.A. Emerton. Leiden: Brill, 1988.

Ovid. *The Fast, Tristia, Pontic Epistles, Ibis, and Halicuticon*, translated by Henry T. Riley. London: H.G. Bohm, 1851.

———. *Metamorphoses*, translated by Frank J. Miller. Loeb Classical Library. Cambridge, MA: Harvard Univ. Press, 1971.

———. *Metamorphoses*, translated by Michael Simpson. Amherst: Univ. of Massachusetts Press, 2001.

———. *Metamorphoses*, translated by Charles Martin. New York: Norton, 2004.

Padel, Ruth. *In and Out of the Mind*. Princeton: Princeton Univ. Press, 1992.

Pagels, Elaine. *Adam, Eve, and the Serpent*. New York: Vintage Books, 1989.

Paglia, Camille. *Sexual Personae*. Reprint. New York: Vintage Books, 1991.

Pahvel, Jaan. *Comparative Mythology*. Baltimore: Johns Hopkins Univ. Press, 1987.

Palache, J. L. *Semantic Notes on the Hebrew Lexicon*. Leiden: Brill, 1959.

Parrot, Andre. *The Arts of Assyria*, translated by Stuart Gilbert and James Emmons. New York: Golden Press, 1961.

Partridge, Eric. *Shakespeare's Bawdy: A Literary and Psychological Essay and a Comprehensive Glossary*. New York: Dutton, 1948.

Pedersen, Johaannes. "The Fall of Man." In *Interpretiones*, edited by N. R. Dahl and A. S. Kapelrud. Oslo: Forlaget Land Ogkirke, 1955.

Pentateuch and Rashi's Commentary, translated by M. Rosenbaum, A. M. Silbermann et al. New York: Hebrew Publishing, n.d.

Perrot, Georges and Charles Chipiez. *A History of Art in Chaldaea and Assyria*. Vol. 1. London: Chapman and Hall, 1884.

Philbrick, Nathaniel. "Quakers with a Vengeance." *Smithsonian* 46, 8 (2015): 18–31.

Plato, *The Dialogues of Plato*, translated by B. Jowett. Vol. 2. New York: Random House, 1937.

Platt, Elizabeth Ellen. "Triangular Jewelry Plaques." *Bulletin of the American Schools of Oriental Research* 221 (1976): 103–11.

Plaut, W. Gunther, translator and commentator *The Torah—Genesis.* New York: Union of American Hebrew Congregations, 1974.

Pliny. *Natural History,* translated by H. Rackham. Loeb Classical Library. Vol. 2. London: William Heinemann, 1947.

Plumb, J. H. *The Death of the Past.* Boston: Houghton Mifflin, 1970.

Plutarch. *Lives,* translated by Bernadotte Perrin. 1st ed., 1919. Loeb Classical Library. Vol. 7. London: William Heinemann, 1928.

———. *Moralia,* translated by Frank C. Babbitt. Loeb Classical Library. Vol. 5. London: William Heinemann, 1936.

Pope, Marvin H. *Job.* Anchor Bible. Garden City: Doubleday, 1965.

———. *Song of Songs.* Anchor Bible. Garden City: Doubleday, 1977.

Popenoe, Paul. "The Propagation of the Date Palm: Materials for a Lexicographical Study in Arabic." *Journal of the American Oriental Society* 35 (1915): 207–12.

Postgate, J. H. *Early Mesopotamia.* London: Routledge, 1992.

Profet, Margie. "Menstruation as a Defense against Pathogens Transported by Sperm." *Quarterly Review of Biology* 68 (1993): 335–88.

Pritchard, James B. *Ancient Near Eastern Texts: Relating to the Old Testament.* 2nd ed. Princeton: Princeton Univ. Press, 1955.

———. *Archeology and the Old Testament.* Princeton: Princeton Univ. Press, 1958.

Pucci, Pietro. *Hesiod and the Language of Poetry.* Baltimore: Johns Hopkins Univ. Press, 1977.

Rabbe, Paul R. "Deliberate Ambiguity in the Psalter." *Journal of Biblical Literature* 110 (1991): 213–27.

Rad, Gerhard von. *Genesis: A Commentary,* Translated by John H. Marks. Philadelphia: Westminster, 1961.

Radday, Yehudah T. and Haim Shore, Moshe A. Pollatschek, and Dieter Wickmann. "Genesis, Wellhausen and the Computer." *Zeitschrift fur die Alttestamentliche Wissenschaft* 94 (1892): 467–89.

———. *Genesis: An Authorship Study in Computer-Assisted Statistical Linguistics.* Rome: Biblical Institute Press, 1985.

Rajak, Tessa. *Translation and Survival: The Greek Bible of the Ancient Jewish Diaspora*. Oxford: Oxford Univ. Press, 2009.

Ray, Dorothy Jean. *Eskimo Art*. Seattle: Univ. of Washington Press, 1977.

Reid, Helen E. "The Brass-Ring Sign." *Lancet*, May 18 (1974): 988.

Reiner, Erica. "The Etiological Myth of the 'Seven Sages.'" *Orientalia* n. s. 30 (1961): 1–11.

Remnick, David. "The Devil Problem." *The New Yorker*, April 3, 1995.

Rendsburg, Gary. "Janus Parallelism in Gen 49:26." *Journal of Biblical Literature* 99 (1980): 291–3.

Ritchie, Ian D. "The Nose Knows: Bodily Knowing in Isaiah 11:3." *Journal for the Study of the Old testament* 87 (1999): 59–73.

Roberts, J. J. M. *The Earliest Semitic Pantheon*. Baltimore: Johns Hopkins Univ. Press, 1972.

Robertson, Edward. "The Apple of the Eye in the Masoretic Text." *Journal of Theolological Studies* 38 (1937): 56–59.

Rowley, H. H. "Zadok and Nehushtan." *Journal of Biblical Literature* 58 (1939): 113–41.

Ruck, Carl A. P. "On the Sacred Names of Iamos and Ion: Ethnobotanical Referents in the Hero's Parentage." *Classical Journal* 71 (1976): 235–52.

Ruiten, J. T. A. G. M. van. "The Intertextual Relationship between Isaiah 65, 25 and Isaiah 11, 6–9." In *The Scriptures and the Scrolls*, edited by F. Garcia Martinez, A. Hilhorst et al. Leiden: Brill, 1992.

Russo, Joseph and Bennett Simon. "Homeric Psychology and the Oral Epic Tradition." *Journal of the History of Ideas* 29 (1968): 438–98.

Sáenz-Badillos, Angel. *A History of the Hebrew Language*, translated by John Elwolde. Cambridge: Cambridge Univ. Press, 1996.

Sandmel, Samuel. *The Hebrew Scriptures: An Introduction to Their Literature and Religious Ideas*. New York: Knopf, 1963.

Sarna, Nahum, translator and commentator. *Genesis—JPS Commentary*. Philadelphia: Jewish Publication Society, 1969.

Sasson, Victor. "The Siloam Tunnel Inscription." *Palestine Exploration Quarterly*, July–December, 1982.

———. "The Aramaic Text of the Tell Fakhrihah Assyrian-Aramaic Bilingual Inscription." *Zeitschrift für die alttestamentliche Wissenschaft* 97 (1985): 86–103.

Sauer, Carl O. *Seeds, Spades, Hearths, and Herds*. Cambridge, MA: MIT Press, 1969.

Saul, Leon J. "Feminine Significance of the Nose." *Psychoanalytic Quarterly* 17 (1949): 51–57.

Scammon. C. M. *The Marine Mammals of the North-western Coast of North America*. Reprint 1969. New York: Dover Publications, 1874.

Scheffer, Victor B. *Seals, Sea Lions, and Walruses*. Stanford: Stanford Univ. Press, 1958.

Schmid, Konrad. "Loss of Immortality? Hermeneutical Aspects of Genesis 2–3 and Its Early Receptions." In *Beyond Eden,* edited by Konrad Schmid and Christoph Riedweg. Tubingen: Mohr Siebeck, 2008.

Schneider, Laurie. "Ms. Medusa: Transformation of a Bisexual Image." In *The Psychoanalytic Study of Society,* edited by Werner Muensterberger and L. Bryce Boyer. Vol. 9. New York: Psychohistory Press, 1981.

Schniedewind, William H. "Textual criticism and Theological Interpretation: The Pro-Temple *Tendenz* in the Greek Text of Samuel–Kings." *Harvard TheologicaL Review* 87 (1994): 107–16.

———. *How the Bible Became a Book*. Cambridge: Cambridge Univ. Press, 2004.

Schottrof, Luise, Silvia Schroer, et al. *Feminist Interpretation: The Bible in Women's Perspective,* translated by Martin and Barbara Rumscheidt. Minneapolis: Fortress, 1998.

Schramm, Brooks. *The Opponents of Third Isaiah*. Sheffield: JSOT Press, 1995.

Schüle, Andreas. "Made in the 'Image of God': The Concepts of Divine Images in Gen 1–3." *Zeitschrift für die Alttestamentliche Wissenschaft* 117 (2005): 1–20.

Schungel-Straumann, Helen. "On the Creation of Man and Woman in Genesis 1–3: The History and Reception of the Texts Considered." In *A Feminist Companion to Genesis,* edited by Athalya Brenner. Sheffield: Sheffield Academic Press, 1993.

Schussler Fiorenza, Elisabeth. *But She Said: Feminist Practices of Biblical Interpretation*. Boston: Beacon Press, 1992.

Schusterman, Ronald J. "Vocal Learning in Mammals with Special Emphasis on Pinnipeds." In *The Evolution of Communicative Creativity*, edited by D. K. Oller and U. Gribel. Cambridge, MA: MIT Press,

Scott, R. B. Y. "The Book of Isaiah." In *The Interpreter's Bible*. Vol. 5. New York: Abingdon Press, 1952.

———. *Proverbs, Ecclesiastes*. Anchor Bible. Garden City: Doubleday, 1965.

———. "Solomon and the Beginnings of Wisdom in Israel." In *Wisdom in Israel and in the Ancient Near East*, edited by M. Noth and D. Winton Thomas. Leiden: Brill, 1969.

Scurlock, J.A. "Magical Uses of Ancient Mesopotamian Festivals of the Dead." In *Ancient Magic and Ritual Power*, edited by Marvin Meyer and Paul Mirecki. Leiden: Brill, 1995.

Segal, Charles P. "The Tragedy of the Hippolytus: The Waters of Ocean and the Untouched Meadow." *Harvard Studies in Classical Philology* 70 (1965).

———. *Tragedy and Civilization*. Cambridge, MA: Harvard Univ. Press, 1981.

Segal, J. B. "Popular Religion in Ancient Israel." *Journal of Jewish Studies* 27 (1976): 1–22.

———. "The Jewish Attitude Towards Women." *Journal of Jewish Studies* 30 (1979): 121–37.

Segal, M. H. "The Religion of Israel before Sinai." *Jewish Quarterly Review* 53 (1963): 226–56.

Shakespeare, William. "King Lear." In *The Riverside Shakespeare*. 2nd edition. Boston: Houghton Mifflin, 1997.

Shanks, Hershel. "Against the Tide: An Interview with Maverick Scholar Cyrus Gordon." *Biblical Archaeology Review* 26 (2000): 52–71.

Shepard, Katherine. *The Fish-Tailed Monster in Greek and Etruscan Art*. New York: privately printed, 1940.

Sheres, Ita. *Dinah's Rebellion: A Biblical Parable for Our Time*. New York: Crossroad Publishing Co., 1990.

Shisler, Famee L. "The Use of Stage Business to Portray Emotion in Greek Tragedy." *American Journal of Philology* 66 (1945): 377–97.

Simon, N. and P. Geroudet. *Last Survivors*. New York: World Publishing, 1970.

Singer, Charles. *A Short History of Anatomy from the Greeks to Harvey*. Originally published as *The Evolution of Anatomy*, 1925. New York: Dover Publications, 1957.

Ska, Jean-Louis. "Genesis 2–3: Some Fundamental Questions." In *Beyond Eden*, edited by Konrad Schmid and Christoph Riedweg. Tubingen: Mohr Siebeck, 2008.

Skehan, Patrick W. and Alexander A. DiLella, translators and commentators. *The Wisdom of Ben Sira*. Anchor Bible. New York: Doubleday, 1987.

Skinner, John. *Genesis: A Critical and Exegetical Commentary*. The International Critical Commentary Series. New York: Scribner, 1917.

Slater, Philip E. *The Glory of Hera: Greek Mythology and the Greek Family*. Boston: Beacon Press, 1968.

Smith, Mark S. *The Early History of God*. San Francisco: Harper & Row, 1990.

———. *The Origins of Biblical Monotheism: Israel's Polytheistic background and the Ugaritic Texts*. New York: Oxford Univ. Press, 2001a.

———. *Untold Stories: The Bible and Ugaritic Studies in the Twentieth Century*. Peabody: Hendrickson, 2001b.

Smith, Morton. *Palestinian Parties and Politics That Shaped the Old Testament*. New York: Columbia Univ. Press. Reprint 1971. London: SCM Press, 1987.

Smith, P. A. *Rhetoric and Redaction in Trito-Isaiah: The Structure, Growth and the Authorship of Isaiah 56–66*. Leiden: Brill, 1995.

Smith, W. Robertson. *The Religion of the Semites*. 2nd ed. 1894. New York: Meridian Books, 1957.

Snell, Bruno. *The Discovery of the Mind*, translated by T. G. Rosenmeyer. Cambridge, MA: Harvard Univ. Press, 1953.

Soggin, Alberto. "The Equality of Humankind from the Perspective of the Creation Stories in Genesis 1: 26–30 and 2: 9, 15, 18–24." *Journal of Northwest Semitic Languages* 23 (1997): 21–33.

Soloveitchik, Joseph B. “The Lonely Man of Faith.” First appeared in *Tradition* 7 (1965): 5–67. New York: Doubleday, 1992.

Sophocles. *Antigone,* translated by Elizabeth Wyckoff. New York: Modern Library, 1942.

———. *The Trachiniae,* translated by R.C. Jebb. Reprint. Amersterdam: Servio Publishers, 1962.

Soren, David, Aicha Ben Abed, et al. *Carthage: Uncovering the Mysteries and Splendors of Ancient Tunisia.* New York: Simon and Schuster, 1990.

Sowers, Sidney G. “Did Xerxes Wage War on Jerusalem?” *Hebrew Union College Annua* 67 (1996): 43–53.

Speiser, E.A. *Genesis.* Anchor Bible. Garden City: Doubleday, 1964.

———. “The Rivers of Paradise.” In *Oriental and Biblical Studies —Collected Writings of E. A. Speiser,* edited by J. J. Finkelstein and Moshe Greenberg. Philadelphia: University of Pennsylvania Press, 1967.

Stadelmann, Luis I. J. *The Hebrew Conception of the World: A Philological and Literary Study.* Rome: Pontifical Biblical Institute, 1970.

Stern, E. “The Archeology of Persian Palestine.” In *The Cambridge History of Judaism,* edited by W.D. Davies and Louis Finkelstein. Cambridge: Cambridge Univ. Press, 1984.

Stordalen, Terje. “Genesis 2, 4. Restudying a *locus classicus.*” *Zeitschrift fur die Alttestamentliche Wissenschaft.”* 104 (1992a): 163–77.

———. “Man, Soil, Garden: Basic Plot in Genesis 2–3 Reconsidered.” *Journal for the Study of the Old Testament* 53 (1992b): 3–26.

Strabo. *Geography,* translated by Horace L. Jones. Loeb Classical Library. Cambridge, MA: Harvard Univ. Press, 1944.

Straus, Erwin W. “The Upright Position.” *Psychiatric Quarterly* 26 (1952): 529–61.

Strauss, Leo. “On the Interpretation of Genesis.” *L'Homme* 21 (1981): 5–20.

Suetonius. *Peri Blasphemion and Peri Paidion,* commentary by Jean Taillardat. Paris: Société d'Edition “Les Belles Lettres,” 1967.

Talmon, S. "Concerning the Documentary Hypothesis in General." In Radday, Shore et al. *Genesis: An Authorship Study in Computer-Assisted Statistical Linguistics*. 1985.

Tatar, Maria. *Off With Their Heads!: Fairy Tales and the Culture of Childhood*. Princeton: Princeton Univ. Press, 1992.

Taylor, Joan E. "The Ashera, the Menorah and the Sacred Tree." *Journal for the Study of the Old Testament* 66 (1995): 29–54.

Thass-Thienemann, Theodore. *The Subconscious Language*. New York: Washington Square Press, 1967.

———. *Symbolic Behavior*. New York: Washington Square Press, 1968.

The Jerusalem Post. International edition. November 1–7, 1981.

Theophrastus. *Enquiry into Plants and Minor Works on Odours and Weather Signs*, tran. Arthur Hort. Loeb Classical Library. 2 vols. London: William Heinemann, 1916.

Thomas, D. Winton. *The Recovery of the Ancient Hebrew Language*. Cambridge: Cambridge Univ. Press, 1939.

———. *Understanding the Old Testament*. London: Athlone Press, 1967.

Thomas, Keith. "History and Anthropology." *Past and Present* 24 (1963): 3–24.

———. "O death, where is thy stink?" *Guardian Weekly*, April 5, 1992.

Thomas, Lewis. *Late Night Thoughts on Listening to Mahler's Ninth Symphony*. New York: Bantam Books, 1984.

Thomasset, Claude. "The Nature of Woman." In *A History of Woman in the West*, edited by Christiane Klupisch-Zuber, translated by Arthur Goldhammer. Vol. 2. Cambridge, MA: Harvard Univ. Press, 1992.

Thomson, David. *People of the Sea: A Journey in Search of the Seal Legend*. 1st ed., 1954. London: Barrie and Rockcliff, 1965.

Toil, H. "Azalea, the Prince of the Steepe: A Comparative Study." *Zeitschrift für die Alttestamentliche Wissenschaft* 92 (1980): 43–59.

Toorn, Karel van der. *Sin and Sanction in Israel and Mesopotamia: A Comparative Study*. Studia Semitica Neerlandica 22. Assen: Van Gorcum, 1985.

———. "Echoes of Judaean Necromancy in Isaiah 28, 7–22." *Zeitschrift für die Alttestamentliche Wissenschaft* 100 (1988): 199–217.

———. *Scribal Culture and the Making of the Hebrew Bible*. Cambridge, MA: Harvard Univ. Press, 2007.

Torczyner, Harry (Tur-Sinai). "How Satan Came into the World." In *Hebrew University Bulletin*, vol. 4 (1937).

———. "Semel Ha-qin'ah Ha-Maqneh." *Journal of Biblical Literature* 65 (1946): 293–302.

Trible, Phyllis. "Depatriarchalizing in Biblical Interpretation." *Journal of the American Academy of Religion* 41 (1973): 30–48.

———. "'Not a Jot, Not a Tittle: Genesis 2–3 after Twenty Years.'" In *Eve and Adam: Jewish, Christian, and Muslim Readings on Genesis and Gender*, edited by Kristan E. Kvam, Linde Schearing, et al. Bloomington: Indiana Univ. Press, 1999.

Tsevat, Matitiahu. "Some Biblical Notes." *Hebrew Union College Annual* 24 (1952): 107–14.

———. "Ishboshet and Congeners: The Names and Their Study." In *Hebrew Union College Annual* 46 (1975): 71–87.

Tsumura, David T. *The Earth and the Waters in Genesis 1 and 2: A Linguistic Investigation*. Sheffield: JSOT Press, 1989.

———. "A Note on (Gen 3, 16)." *Biblica* 75 (1994): 398–400.

Tur-Sinai, N.H. *The Book of Job: A New Commentary*. Jerusalem: Kiryath Sepher, 1957.

Twain, Mark. *Extracts from Adam's Diary*. New York: Harper and Brothers, 1906.

Ullendorff, Edward. *The Bawdy Bible*. Oxford: Oxford Centre for Postgraduate Hebrew Studies, 1978.

Updike, John. *Villages*. New York: Knopf, 2004.

Vaughn, Andrew G. *Theology, History, and Archeology in the Chronicler's Account of Hezekiah*. Atlanta: Scholars Press, 1999.

Vaux, Roland de. *Ancient Israel: Its Life and Institutions*, translated by John McHugh. New York: McGraw-Hill, 1961.

Veenker, Ronald A. *Forbidden Fruit: Ancient Near Eastern Sexual Metaphors*. Bowling Green, KY: Western Kentucky Univ, 1994.

Vegetti, Mario. "The Greeks and Their Gods." In *The Greeks*, edited by Jean-Pierre Vernant, translated by Charles Lambert and Teresa Lavender Fagan. Chicago: Univ. of Chicago Press, 1995.

Vermeule, Emily. "The World Turned Upside Down." *The New York Review of Books* 39, 6 (1992): 40–3.

Vernant, Jean-Pierre. *Mortals and Immortals: Collected Essays*, edited by Froma I. Zeitlin. Princeton: Princeton Univ. Press, 1991.

Vidal-Naquet, Pierre. *Assassins of Memory*, translated by Jeffrey Mehlman. New York: Columbia Univ. Press, 1992.

Viagra (sildenafil citrate) product information. New York: Pfizer Inc., March 1998.

Virgil. *Aeneid*, translated by H. R. Fairclough. 1st ed., 1918. Loeb Classical Library. Cambridge, MA: Harvard Univ. Press, 1953.

Vroon, Piet. *Smell*, translated by Paul Vincent. New York: Farrar, Straus and Giroux, 1997.

Wakeman, Mary. *God's Battle with the Monster*. Leiden: Brill, 1973.

Wallace, Howard. N. *The Eden Narrative*. Atlanta: Scholars Press, 1985.

Walters, Stanley D. "Hannah and Anna: The Greek and Hebrew Texts of 1 Samuel 1." *Journal of Biblical Literature*, 107 (1988): 385–412.

Walzer, Michael. *In God's Shadow: Politics in the Hebrew Bible*. New Haven: Yale Univ. Press, 2012.

Watson, Wilfred G.E. *Classical Hebrew Poetry: A Guide to its Techniques*. Sheffield: JSOT Press, 1984.

Webster's Third International Dictionary. 4th ed., 1961. Springfield, MA: Merriam, 1976.

Weinberg, Werner. "Transliteration and Transcription of Hebrew," *Hebrew Union College Annual* 40-41 (1969-70): 1-32

Weinfeld, Moshe. "Deuteronomy—The Present State of Inquiry." *Journal of Biblical Literature* 86 (1967): 249–62.

———. *Deuteronomy and the Deuteronomic School*. Oxford: Clarendon Press, 1972.

Weingreen, J. *Introduction to the Critical Study of Text of the Hebrew Bible*. Oxford: Clarendon Press, 1982.

Wellhausen, Julius. *Prolegomena to the History of Ancient Israel.* Meridian Books, 4th printing, 1965. Cleveland: World Publishing Co., 1878.

Wenham, G. J. "Genesis: An Authorship Study and Current Pentateuchal Criticism." *Journal for the Study of the Old Testament* 42 (1988): 3–18.

Westermann, Claus. *Genesis 1–11,* Translated by John J. Scullion. Minneapolis: Augsburg, 1984; Minneapolis: Fortress Press, 1994.

Westropp, Thomas J. "A Folklore Survey of County Clare." *Folklore* 22 (1911): 449–56.

White, John B. A *Study of the Language of Love in the Song of Songs and Ancient Egyptian Poetry*. Missoula: Scholars Press, 1978.

Whybray, R.N. "Isaiah 40–66." *New Century Bible Commentary.* Grand Rapids: Eerdman's, 1981.

Wiener, Norbert. *God and Golem, Inc.* Cambridge, MA: M. I. T. Press, 1966.

Wilbur, George B. "The Reciprocal Relationship of Man and His Ideological Milieu." *American Imago* 3 (1946): 3–48.

Wilford, John Noble. "Long-Lost Field Notes Help Decode Treasure." *New York Times,* September 21, 1993.

Williams, Bernard. *Shame and Necessity*. Berekely: Univ. of California Press, 1993.

Williams, R. J. "'A People Come Out of Egypt': An Egyptologist Looks at the Old Testament." In *Supplements to Vetus Testamentum*. Vol. 28, edited by J.A. Emerton. Leiden: Brill, 1975.

Williams, Tennessee. "Cat on a Hot Tin Roof." In *Theatre '55,* edited by John Chapman. New York: Random House, 1955.

Williamson, H. G. M. *Word Biblical Commentary: Ezra, Nehemia.* Waco: Word Books, 1985.

Winkler, John J. *The Constraints of Desire*. New York: Routledge, 1990.

Wolff, Hans Walter. *Anthropology of the Old Testament,* translated by Margaret Kohl. Philadelphia: Fortress, 1974.

Wood, Francis A. "Etymological Miscellany." *American Journal of Philology* 21 (1900): 178–82.

———. "Etymological Notes." *Modern Language Notes* 17 (1902): 3–6.

Yadin, Yigael. *The Art of Warfare in Biblical Lands*. Vol. 1. New York: McGraw-Hill, 1963.

Yahuda, A.S. "The Meaning of the Name Esther." *Journal of the Royal Asiatic Society*, 1946: 174–78.

Yee, Gale A. "I Have Perfumed My Bed with Myrrh: The Foreign Woman (iŝŝa zara) in Proverbs 1–9." *Journal for the Study of the Old Testament* 43 (1989): 53–68.

Zevit, Ziony. "The Khirbet el-Qom Inscription Mentioning a Goddess." *Bulletin of the American Schools of Oriental Research*, no. 255 (1984): 39–47.

———. *What Really Happened in the Garden of Eden*? New Haven: Yale University Press, 2013.

Zuntz, Gunther. *Persephone*. Oxford: Clarendon Press, 1971.

INDEX

Q

R

S

BIBLICAL INDEX

CPSIA information can be obtained
at www.ICGtesting.com
Printed in the USA
LVHW110322060721
691957LV00003B/143/J